BEFORE
HISTORY
DIES

BEFORE HISTORY DIES

By

JACOB M. CARTER

WordCrafts

Published by WordCrafts Press
Buffalo, WY 82834
www.wordcrafts.net

of half truths. We don't want to sit at the table and play the "Who killed JFK" trivia game any longer. The Who's Who of shooters, mixed with the mass confusion that social media forums provide, has left us Millennials doing what we do best…not caring.

This is where my conviction springs from. I want to be a voice of reason for my generation, because as crazy as it seems, I believe President Kennedy's assassination still affects us today. The results of Dealey plaza had a major historical impact on our society, and those events still shade our attitudes in both large and small ways that we might not even be aware of. I believe this is where our modern skepticism originated from in the first place.

A few years back I was just like most of the people in my generation - I didn't give a flip who killed JFK. I thought it was boring, a waste of my time. I had a family member who taught college-level history, which cultivated my love for the subject as a younger child. But by my teenage years I had bought into the progressive lie that history had become irrelevant. It was not until I was nearly 20 years old that I started to notice the effects this worldview had on my thinking.

One night, while surfing the TV for a movie, I stumbled upon Oliver Stone's Oscar-winning film, 'JFK.' I was hooked. As soon as the credits rolled, I booted up my computer for a fact-check session. History started to come to life for me, and I began to understand the weight this assassination played on the American story.

This process started slowly for me. I spent hours upon hours reading documents and chewing on old documentaries. There were times I questioned if it was all a waste of time, but the mystery of this case kept me pursuing its many twists and turns until I got a good grasp on the basics.

I followed this season up by getting lost in the forest of conspiracy theories. It took me years of wandering through those thick trees before I finally found the path of sound logic again. After experiencing that, I decided to step away from the internet forums and go directly to the experts themselves. This was the best decision I made because it educated me on the case in a way I couldn't get by just reading blogs.

When all was said and done, I was shocked by how misleading many of the assassination books could be. I learned that history, if not fact checked, can be rewritten with smooth words and cunning edits.

Simply put, a lot of the conspiracy theories were created through clever lies.

And yet…many alternatives to these conspiracy theories seemed like they simply brushed the more troubling questions aside. I could not believe in a massive worldwide conspiracy to murder JFK, but I also could not explain why the government repeatedly lied to its own citizens on such an important topic.

It alarmed me that so many people I knew were so disinterested in historical facts. If our government would lie to us about the JFK assassination, what else could we be lied to about, if those in power believed we didn't care?

That is why I wrote this book. I am convinced that President Kennedy's assassination was the key point in our history that led us to this cynical society we live in today. I hope this work can make a tiny dent in the apathetic approach to history that has been created in the post-JFK world.

I don't expect it to be easy. The Kennedy assassination has a legacy of disinformation and ignorance, but that doesn't mean we shouldn't try to understand it. This case is still an ongoing battle today. Right now there are thousands of documents pertaining to the assassination that are locked away in vaults and filing cabinets all over the world. I hope this thought might appeal to your skeptical nature. Is there any legitimate reason we shouldn't have access to those documents? Shouldn't we, as citizens, be able to see all of these documents in full?

If no one asks to see them, will they just languish away until we fade away? Will we allow history to die with all these questions unresolved? I hope not. As the old saying goes, those who will not learn from the past are doomed to repeat it. We need to understand our past to prevent it from happening again.

According to ABC News, there have been more than 2,000 books written about JFK's assassination. Some are pretty good, others are misleading at best. In any case, there is no shortage of information available to any interested reader. I did not want to just write another JFK book with regurgitated information and call it "my book." Instead, I decided to interview some of the world's top researchers from both sides of the debate, and allow readers to come to their own conclusions.

Instead of writing another book on another theory, I hoped to save my readers the time I wasted by following the wrong researchers. In short, I wanted to provide a book that could be a research tool for people who want to study history on their own terms.

I interviewed experts and adherents of the Lone Assassin theory (Oswald acted alone) and of the Conspiracy theory (Oswald was a pawn in a greater conspiracy). I tried to be respectful of the researchers on both sides who allowed me to interview them. Some many not agree with this approach, but I believe it is important to understand and consider both sides of any case if you seek to have your mind settled on it. I think the result will be a book that can be a great asset in your search for the truth.

I think John F. Kennedy was a special President. He had his flaws, but he had a passion for America and an overall view of a better world for humankind. He saved us from a nuclear war, and he set the standard for what a true statesman should look like. I think we owe it to his legacy to set the record of his assassination as straight as we can, and to try to answer the biggest question mark in American history.

I hope this book will help you in this challenge. It is left up to our generation to research this case, and then to educate the next generation behind us…before history dies.

The Conspiracy Theory

I cannot blame people for believing in a conspiracy when it comes to the assassination of President Kennedy. Lee Harvey Oswald, although poor and mentally disturbed, was no ordinary "crack pot." At a young age, he left the Marine Corps and attempted to defect to the Soviet Union, America's communist arch-enemy at the time. He soon returned to America with a Russian wife at his side, and he openly supported Cuba's communist leader, Fidel Castro, by handing out pro-Cuba leaflets on America's street corners. He had contact with individuals who had distant intelligence ties. He traveled to Mexico City to get a visa to Cuba, and the photos the CIA had of him there simply vanished after the fact.

Soon thereafter, he returned to Dallas and murdered the leader of the free world.

Oswald denied all guilt for this crime, and was gunned down on live television by a shady nightclub owner while he was surrounded by Dallas police officers. In light of that storyline, do you have to be nuts to be suspicious? I don't think so.

Some of the most credible Conspiracy Theory advocates I could find raise excellent arguments for just such a conspiracy. They leave us wondering why the government has responded to the assassination in such a strange, if not outright deceitful, manner. They point out the controversy involving President Kennedy's wounds. They present their views regarding how many shooters might have been in Dealey Plaza, and why the CIA has been so reluctant to cooperate with any investigation into the matter. And they offer their opinions about why a murder from half a century before should still matter to us today.

Was there a conspiracy to murder the President? Why has the government withheld assassination related documents for over a period of 50-plus years? Did Lee Harvey Oswald act on orders to murder the President, or was he set up to take the fall? Did Jack Ruby murder Lee Harvey Oswald to silence him? If so, who sent him to do the job? These experts believe they have solid answers to these questions. Let's see if that is the case.

Jefferson Morley

Jefferson Morley is a former Washington Post reporter and a respected JFK assassination researcher. He is the founder of JFKfacts.org, a website dedicated to fact-checking all of the aspects that surround the assassination, and author of the book, *Our Man in Mexico: Winston Scott and the Hidden History of the CIA.* After spending years getting burned by conspiracy theorists, I stumbled upon Jefferson Morley's work through other authors. What separated Mr. Morley from other "researchers" was his logical approach to the question of conspiracy, and his willingness to not adhere to theories if the evidence didn't support them. Mr. Morley also has a unique experience in battling the CIA for their remaining documents on the JFK assassination. This, among many other reasons, is why I wanted the reader to hear Mr. Morley's perspective.

In the History channel documentary, "JFK Assassination: The Definitive Guide," you said, "...suspicions of conspiracy did not originate with conspiracy theorists, they did not begin with Oliver Stone. Suspicions of a conspiracy originated in the circumstances of the crime." Can you please explain what you meant by that?

Well, some people say, "the President was shot and everyone knew what had happened, and then conspiracy theorists came along later and drummed up these theories." In fact, what happened was when people saw and learned about what occurred in the assassination, they immediately came to the conclusion that one person couldn't have done this. So, it wasn't that someone later on wrote an article or a book or published a movie that put forth a conspiracy theory and the only motive was that these people were trying to sell something.

Instead, it was the facts themselves. It was the facts of the events that made people question what happened. So, I was trying to draw a distinction between when people say that Oliver Stone just conned people into believing a conspiracy theory. No, it doesn't work that way. It was the facts of the crime that made people think it happened in a different way than the way the Warren Report set forth. That's what I was trying to say.

Could you please tell us about Lee Harvey Oswald and his possible ties to the American intelligence community?

Well, I think what we have learned, especially through the work of the Assassination Record Review Board, we have a much fuller record of what the CIA knew about Oswald. We now know they knew much more about him than they ever told the Warren Commission. He was very well known to a number of high ranking officials in the intelligence community. That's not a theory, that's a fact.

From the day he entered the Soviet Union in October 1959, until the day he died in November of 1963, there were four years that the CIA collected information on Oswald constantly. By the time he died, they had about 40 to 50 reports on him in their CIA file. From the State Department, from the FBI, from the CIA itself, they had intercepted his mother's correspondent. They knew who this guy was.

This idea that some guy came out of nowhere to kill the President isn't true. If Oswald did kill the President, then it was done by a guy who the CIA knew about before hand. And so, that raises the question of what was the nature of their interest? Were they looking to get intelligence from him? Were they manipulating him? It was an unusual level of attention that he got. It wasn't like a normal or routine check. Was he some kind of intelligent asset? Now, there's no way to prove that, but there's a lot that says it may be the case.

The Warren Commission could never establish how Oswald got to Finland to enter the Soviet Union. I mean, here's a guy who's a high school drop out, and he's 20 years old, and he figures out that he's going to go to the only place in the world where he could get a visa at that time. If he had gone any other place in the world, he would not have got into the Soviet Union that quickly. How did Oswald know to go to Helsinki? That's one question, and another one is how did he get there? No one has answered these questions, leading some to speculate he was taken there on a U.S. military plane. That's speculative, but it's certainly possible based on the undisputed evidence that we have. That's where it seems like he was enjoying some level of protection.

How about the infamous J. Edgar Hoover/LBJ phone call? Did it concern Oswald's intelligence connections as well?

Well, the fact that Oswald was so well known by the CIA was shocking to officials. They were indeed concerned about these connections immediately after the assassination, and quickly started to suppress those connections at high levels. They were largely successful in keeping them out of the Warren Commission's findings. Now, did Hoover and LBJ talk about that? I don't know, maybe. But that would be pure speculation.

In light of all you know, do you think the CIA was complicit in the assassination, or do you think they were just protecting their self-interest afterwards?

I think people in the CIA were responsible for the assassination, let's put it that way. That's not to say there was a conspiracy to murder the President, because I can't point to any individual member of a conspiracy.

But the assassination of the President was an intelligence failure. The U.S. government should have had sufficient information to prevent that from happening. The government failed. Where did the failure originate? It originated in the CIA. It was the malfeasance of the CIA that caused the wrongful death of the President, whether Oswald did it alone, or he was apart of a conspiracy.

In light of that, why do you believe that the CIA is so reluctant to release the

George Joannides file? Is there a connection to the failure of the CIA, Joannides, and the murder of the President?

I think that there was a covert operation, an on-the-rise covert operation that involved Oswald. It was approved by CIA officials, and that's what they can't admit. That's not to say the operation was a plot to kill the President. I'm not sure of that, but I'm pretty sure there was an operation around Oswald to manipulate him and discredit the Fair Play for Cuba Committee.

CIA officials reporting to Dick Helms, the Deputy Director, and James Angleton, the Counterintelligence Chief, were responsible for that operation, and that's what they want to hide. Now, Joannides was relatively low down in that operation. He was a secondary figure. It wasn't his idea. He wasn't a major player in it, but he assisted in it and that's why they can't release his file. It would be embarrassing to the agency, and would destroy their official story on Oswald.

But aren't we facing the inevitable here? I mean, won't that eventually happen anyway?

You know, I'd like to think so. I think people are aware of it. There are forces for disclosures out there, but they could destroy the files. I don't think they ever thought people would snuff this stuff out. The only hope we have is that it was too late to destroy them, and that people realize that if they were destroyed, it would be a crime. It's a crime to destroy a federal record without authorization. So, I do hope those records will come out in the next few years.

Let me ask you about Mexico. Who was impersonating Oswald in Mexico, if indeed he was being impersonated? Also, who was the man in the pictures that the CIA said was Oswald....who clearly wasn't?

Well, to answer the second question first, there were people in the CIA who identified that person as someone who had contact with the Soviet embassy in Mexico City. I don't think that person had anything to do with the assassination. I think they were thrown into the mix to confuse and confound the Soviet Union, and make them look bad.

Now, as to who impersonated Oswald, I think it was someone connected to the CIA. I say that because the CIA did run impersonation operations around the Cuban embassy in Mexico City, and we have records of one of them. What they would do is when someone would go into the Cuban embassy they would overhear them talking, and when they would leave, the CIA would call the Cuban embassy and act as if they were that visiting individual. Take for instance, a man would go into the Cuban embassy and offer to run guns for Castro, and then leave. The CIA would then call the man who went into the Cuban embassy and say, "we understand you want to help Castro, please come and meet us, but don't go anywhere near the embassy." They pretended to be Cuban government officials and went to talk with this person. So, impersonation was a tactic that espionage people used.

Now, what the evidence shows is that someone called the Soviet embassy speaking very poor Russian, trying to claim that they were Oswald, and wanted to talk with the embassy officials. However Oswald spoke pretty good Russian, so this was someone impersonating him. It was probably someone within the CIA - on the point of view of trying to learn something about the Soviet Union. That's why you do an impersonation operation, to see how the enemy reacts. That's probably what was going on, but as to who that was, we don't know.

Going further on the Mexico incident, what do you make of Silvia Odio, and her testimony of meeting Oswald? What about the contradictions on the timeline, some placing Oswald on a bus going to Mexico City and some placing Oswald in her apartment with two anti-Castro Cubans at that time?

I think it did happen. Silvia never did pinpoint an exact date. It is possible Oswald went there, and got on the bus the next day. The bulk of the evidence indicates it did happen. I felt like her identification of Oswald, and her sister's as well, was strong. It was reported contemporaneously, and she had spoken to her psychiatrist about the event when it happened. So, there was a lot of collaborating evidence backing her story up.

What about the two anti-Castro Cubans Oswald was with in Odio's apartment? If it's true he was with them, and the next day got on a bus to try and enter Cuba, is that not proof of a conspiracy?

Yeah, it's not proof of a criminal act, but I do find it strange that a guy who was a liberal and leftist in his political views was hanging out with David Ferrie, who was very anti-JFK, and very anti-Castro. Oswald was an open admirer of Castro, and he was not terribly critical of JFK. There was nothing Oswald said about hating JFK.

As matter of fact, Oswald was anti-racist. He acted that way. When he went to court in New Orleans he sat with the segregated blacks. That's how he was. The idea that Oswald hated Kennedy isn't very plausible. So, the fact that Oswald was with some very conservative, anti-JFK people lends credence to what Oswald said….that he was a patsy and had been set up by the enemies of the President.

I have spoken with some who say people can't handle the fact that a loser like Oswald killed a grand individual like President Kennedy, therefore we desire a conspiracy. What do you have to say about this psychological evaluation in light of all the evidence on the case that you have seen?

If we're going to the question of psychological motivation, it's equally plausible that people want to deny a conspiracy because it's unsettling. It would prove that people got away with the crime, or our government failed, and the media failed, and people don't want to admit that. You can say that people don't want to admit that either. So, those two arguments are equally plausible, and can be made for either side, and I don't think it's a very strong point.

Here's a devil's advocate question when it comes to a conspiracy. In order for Oswald to be manipulated, or to be apart of a conspiracy, he needed to be put inside the book depository, and we know Oswald got the job via Ruth Paine. If this is the case, how could there have been any assurance for the conspirators that Oswald would have been in that building on November 22nd?

Yeah, I mean, that's a good question. If there was a conspiracy, how did they get Oswald into the schoolbook depository? It's not exactly true that Ruth Paine got Oswald the job. She referred him to the Texas Employment Commission, which got him the job. He had other job opportunities at the time, but he didn't take them. I don't pretend to have all the answers, but it's a good question.

What do you make of the medical evidence? Do you believe it?

There's a big contradiction between what most of the people in Dallas saw, which was a blow out wound consistent with the President being hit in the temple, and a wound in the back of his head, and what the doctors saw in Bethesda. I mean, I can't resolve it, but you can't wish it away either.

Take Dr. McClelland for example. He was standing right over the President, and gazing at that wound for ten minutes, so I don't question what he saw. And, the autopsy was done in peculiar circumstances; military officers controlled it. One of the FBI agents who was in there said surgery had been done on the head before the autopsy. So, the wound could have been manipulated before the autopsy took place, and I believe that's what probably happened.

Do you believe in the magic bullet theory?

No, and it's important to realize that nobody in the limousine believed in the magic bullet theory. Not Jackie Kennedy, not John Connolly, not Nellie Connolly. They all said the first bullet hit the President in the back, the second hit John Connolly in the back, the third hit the President in the head.

The idea that one bullet caused those wounds, it's not plausible. It's not consistent with the Zapruder film, it's not consistent with the eyewitness testimony, and it's not what anyone at the crime thought had happened. It was something that was thought up later to rationalize the idea that Oswald did it alone, so the evidence was fit into theory, and the theory didn't emerge from the evidence.

Why does the Kennedy assassination matter in this day and time?

If we look at the power of the National Security Agency today we see the effects from the assassination. We see them abusing their power in their mass surveillance of the people, exercising power beyond the constitution. That's our reality today. But how did that come to be? Well, these agencies got their power after World War Two, and during the Cold War, and the JFK assassination was a time where they could have been held accountable and they weren't. So, it matters today because I think that's when the CIA and other National Security agencies consolidated their power beyond the reach of the law.

That's not say all these agencies got together and said, *we're going to kill President Kennedy*. I don't think that happened. I think that a faction within those agencies conspired to kill the President, but we really don't know what happened. I do know the President's enemies wanted him dead and he died.

I don't know if Oswald did it, but if he did, it was because he was allowed to. So, if we want to have real self-government, we have to come to terms with this crime. If not, the lawlessness will continue. These agencies will continue to feel like they don't need to obey the law, and that they can do what they want. That's a dangerous situation. That's not self-government. That's an authoritarian system that doesn't belong to the people. The Kennedy assassination was able to change the government without an election, without the will of the people.

Isn't it ridiculous that more than 50 years after the fact, the government claims that they can't reveal certain files to us due to national security?

It's ridiculous. It's suspicious. It's deeply suspicious.

What about those who say the CIA isn't hiding anything important, just covering their self-interest?

If what they're hiding can be made public, and there's nothing there, we will go away. But until they do that, there's no reason to say they aren't hiding something sinister. That's just silly. There's a lot of malfeasance in the case. Evidence has been destroyed and false testimony has been given. The truth was covered up. We can't just say what they're covering up isn't important. It's not important? Come on, that's ridiculous.

Do you ever think that Oswald could have acted alone?

It's very complicated that we don't have a good explanation as to what happened. The explanation we have, which isn't strong, is that Oswald did it and that's the end of it. But we don't know that's true because we haven't had transparency, and the agency is still being secretive about it. We're left in a state where it's difficult to make a definitive statement. But that doesn't mean that it's not serious information or that we can't find out the truth. That's why we need to try.

Where is the JFK case headed now?

There are files that are out there that we have never seen. There are also a lot of materials in the files that have been released that are still redacted, and we need to get the rest of those as well. And finally, where we're going is that we need to understand the CIA's relationship with Oswald better, and that's where we're at. There are existing records that can shed light on that, and I believe if we get them we will understand the assassination better.

Are you finding any success in prying new files from the government's hands?

I have obtained some important information from my lawsuit, and I'm going write about those in my next book, so my lawsuit has had success. I think we have a shot of getting the files in 2017, and I hope we get them. I think the media will put pressure on them, and because of this extra attention on them, they will be forced to release those files. But, they're in a powerful position, and it's very difficult to challenge them in court, so it remains to be seen, but I'm hopeful.

What happened on Nov. 22nd, 1963?

I think the President was ambushed by his enemies. These were people who feared his foreign policy, and saw the President himself as a threat to the United States. I think that they had him killed. I'm not sure, but that's my opinion.

Do you have any closing remarks?

The Kennedy assassination isn't just history; it's still with us and we still need our government to be held accountable for their lack of transparency in the case. I think the Kennedy assassination is a symbol of the people's fear of our own government, and I think those fears are justified.

Anthony Summers:

As an international investigative reporter, Anthony Summers is a pioneer within the JFK research community. Some of his historic work on this case dates back to the late 1970s, when the government had reopened the assassination for further investigation. He has personally interviewed a host of rarely seen witnesses, and has also discovered evidence that had been previously cloaked in mystery.

Mr. Summer's perspective on this case is unique because he did not work for the American media at the time of his reporting. This enabled him to bring an objective, yet balanced set of eyes to the harder questions about President Kennedy's murder. I highly suggest him to anyone who might be interested in studying this case.

When I was studying the assassination, Mr. Summer's work cleared a lot of smoke out the air for me. His book, *Not in Your Lifetime*, is what some refer to as the Bible of JFK literature. It shows us how to study both sides of the assassination with a critical eye, and then how to draw our own conclusions base on the evidence we have in front of us.

This interview will carry that same spirit, and it will also have something to say to the younger generation about the importance of understanding JFK's murder today.

What is your expertise in the JFK assassination research field?

You should know something of my background. I had been a student at Oxford University, working in a bar, the evening - British time - the news broke in November 1963. Soon after we heard the news, in a radio bulletin, the radio news said the President had been killed, and - while everyone present was standing around stunned - the editor of a prominent television program I had worked for during vacations - a man I held in awe, called me. He said he was chartering a plane to go to Dallas immediately - an extraordinary initiative in 1963. Could I join his team?

This was an amazing opportunity for the young fellow I was then, and I of course said yes at once. He told me to get a taxi to Heathrow Airport, a 50-mile ride, but just as I was getting into the cab the editor's secretary rang me back to say they had found someone more experienced than I.

So, that was how Anthony Summers wound up *not* covering the assassination.

The months and years slipped by, and I sort of followed the story. Mark Lane, the first author to question the official version of the story, came to the UK and made an extraordinary, unimpressive, undignified, shameful appearance on British television. I was deeply underwhelmed, but continued to keep an eye on developments like most of my contemporaries, but probably more than most because I had by then become a journalist in the British Broadcasting Corporation. I had a special interest in investigations, and was spending a lot of time in the United States.

Then, in the late 1960s, came the Garrison trial in New Orleans, which seemed to me to be a circus. Hard for you to imagine, perhaps, because you're young, but in those years only a few serious independent researchers were studying the assassination. There was no Internet then, and people were exchanging views largely by writing those old-fashioned things called 'letters.' There were a few serious people doing that, a number of eccentrics, and some who were downright nut-cases. It was hard to see through the smoke, and I thought the JFK case was a subject to stay the hell away from.

In 1976, though, when it seemed likely that the House Assassinations Committee was going to produce a conspiracy finding - which in the event turned out to be a "probable conspiracy" finding - I got a call from a producer in the U.S. asking whether the BBC wanted to make a documentary. The working title was to be *What Do We Know Now That We Didn't Know*. They did, and I was asked to direct it. This was around 1978.

I took on the assignment, spending many weeks on the road in the United States, particularly in Dallas and New Orleans. I was just appalled at the standard of the reporting, or rather the lack of reporting, there had been by the American media. People imagine the case had been covered really well by the mainstream media, or any media, but it simply hadn't. I found people who were mainstream witnesses that nobody had talked to, and - if they didn't throw me down the stairs - there were people saying to me, "Come on in, why has no one called me before?" And I would apologize, saying, "Surely the FBI talked with you," or "surely the New York Times came and talked to you?" In many cases, no one had talked to them, or had talked with them only superficially, and the documentary gave some of them a voice.

I thought the coverage of the case by the media had been shameful and as I had more information in my notebooks and on tape than I could possibly get into a TV documentary, I thought I might do a book. I was phasing out of the BBC at the time, so I did the book.

I went back to Dallas, and very fortunately was given access to the files of an extraordinary woman named Mary Ferrell, who had got hold of files and pursued material no one else had. While numerous people now gone were still alive, I was able to track them down and talk with them. I went to Mexico City and interviewed numerous witnesses no reporter had previously seen. I went to Cuba, which Americans weren't able to do.

My book was published as *Conspiracy*, not that I was convinced at the time that Kennedy had died as the result of a conspiracy. I'm not entirely convinced of that now, all these years later. When the book was originally being discussed with the publisher, I had voiced the idea that the title could be *Probable Conspiracy*, only to have that notion rejected out of hand by my editor. He said, "Probable conspiracy wouldn't work at all. We're going to call it *Conspiracy*," and *Conspiracy* it became.

I thought, 'I'm going to be labeled as a conspiracy theorist for the rest of my career,' by miraculously escaped that fate. Later, I went down the road and did another documentary, and in the meantime got further into the David Phillips/Maurice Bishop matter, which remains important and unresolved to this day. I did a new updated edition of the book in 1998, then again in 2013. So I think, along the way, I have gained a certain expertise.

Because of your first hand knowledge on the case, along with your work on your book, do you believe the evidence leans more towards a conspiracy, or do you think Lee Oswald did it alone?

The very beginning of my journalistic training, other than when I was a student, was with the SBC, the Swiss Broadcasting Corporation. Switzerland, as you know, is a neutral country and their news coverage was indeed neutral. You can hardly say a single decisive thing about a major event without quoting one side and the other side and then possibly the third and fourth sides. It was after that that I went to the BBC, which certainly at that time had a global reputation for integrity, and I try to maintain that standard, if that does not sound too pompous, in my working life.

It would be wrong for me, and in truth for anyone else, too say that one knows for sure that there was a conspiracy. In my book, I've written carefully that there are real problems with the work of the Warren Commission. The fact is that nobody knows what happened.

One of the reasons I said I would talk with you was that I admired your explanation of what you were trying to do. You said you were particularly keen to get information to young people, so that a younger generation - if they are open to factual information - could gain a real insight into this important piece of modern history. To my own children, the Kennedy assassination is further away than the Second World War was for me when I was growing up. Young people need to know that chunk of history has not been properly reported, was not properly reported by the people who serve the public in the media in the United States, nor indeed by your national agencies, by which I principally mean the FBI and CIA. Almost all of them failed the American people, as former Warren Commission attorney Burt Griffin told me, in multiple ways.

There may perhaps be innocuous reasons behind that failure - an instruction by Kennedy's successor, Johnson, issued because of a perceived danger of nuclear war with a foreign country. Until we definitely know that to be the case, though, it's not enough to settle back and accept that concept.

There certainly was a failure of intelligence agencies across the board, and a failure of the American media, and people need to understand that. Even if the Kennedy assassination doesn't matter to your generation, it does matter that your generation sees the need for genuine work by your law enforcement agencies today, and whenever the next world-shaking event happens. You know the old saying: "If you ignore history, it will repeat itself."

What advice would you have for future researchers investigating this case?

Well, there's a Freedom of Information Act, crippled though it is in many ways. There's been an enormous ongoing effort by people fighting for information that has been withheld. There are a significant number of documents on the Kennedy case, still withheld today on the grounds of national security. If Oswald did it alone with his bow and arrow on November 22, 1963, its nonsense - seems nonsense - that we cannot see everything in the files.

Everything has changed since 1963. America has changed and the Communist world particularly has changed. One so-called justification of having concealed aspects of what happened in Mexico City has been that the United States had Mexico's cooperation of in tapping foreign embassy telephones and surveillance. To reveal the detail of that, it has been suggested, would endanger U.S. relations with Mexico. Perhaps that was so in 1963 and perhaps it was for years afterward, but no sensible person can think that it would endanger America's relationship with Mexico in 2015.

What do you know about David Atlee Phillips?

A lot, and because of the nature of the CIA and of the man himself, not much at all. I appeared on NBC's Today program on NBC with David Phillips, and he was furious over what I had written of references to him in the House Assassinations Committee's volumes. I then tried to approach him to let him have his say in a future edition of the book, but he wouldn't talk me.

As a senior CIA officer, he had in 1963 been involved in much Agency activity related to the secret war against Castro's Cuba. The truth about his role in Mexico City, and specifically in connection with Oswald's alleged visits to Communist diplomatic missions, remains elusive.

Former Assassination Committee investigator Dan Hardway, with whom I believe you have contact, and others who worked with him, can tell you more about that. You absolutely must also read the book *The Last Investigation* by my friend the late Gaeton Fonzi, a terrific investigator and a very brave guy. There are real questions about what David Phillips was up to. I don't know what he was concealing, but that's an area that demands more real digging.

Who do you think might have been involved in the assassination, if there was indeed a conspiracy?

My book doesn't say that I think that the CIA as such was involved in the assassination - not at all. Nor does it say the Mafia did it. On the contrary, I hope you noticed that I question seriously reports that the two Mafia bosses most often mentioned, Trafficante and Marcello, confessed to having been involved in later life in the assassination. They may have been, and if there were any useful testimony or events, I would have laid it out in my book.

There are real questions, real unknowns, though, about organized crime's possible role. And about what some individuals in the CIA or linked to the CIA may have done. I'm not closed, meanwhile, to the theory that Castro's Cuba was involved in the assassination, but I have seen no good evidence to that effect.

This goes back somewhat to your first question - as to my "expertise." What I have done, my analysis aside, has been to see and talk to some of these people. Now, witnesses may of course be deceptive. If you've been on the road a long time as a reporter, though, doing interviews with people, you do get a sense of whether they are leveling with you or whether they are not. It's not a perfect craft by any stretch, but one does come away with a sort of nose-tapping sense of whether you have been given truthful answers or not, or whether someone is telling you half the truth.

My sense of it, from talking with people in this case - across the board - is that something was concealed. No reporter or historian, no one to whom history matters, should be satisfied until they have got as close to the bottom of an issue as possible. Today, the statements of survivors of 1963, or even of the later investigations, can be merely interesting, like sort of chaff on the wind of history.

What one needs most of all is to get to any remaining hard evidence or authentic information that we may not yet have seen - and there may be some. We know that documents are still withheld in the National Archives. In 2015, that is surely nonsense. It's got to be released, and that is what I think you and the new generation of interested citizens should push for.

At the beginning of your book you ask the question, 'Does the assassination of President Kennedy still matter?' Why does it still matter now to Americans?

As I said earlier, if you ignore history you're doomed to repeat it. If things have been hidden from a people then that people becomes dulled to the importance of that elusive thing we humans call "Truth." Given that there is good evidence on the Kennedy assassination that has been concealed, and that there has been deception - and given that it occurred a mere half century ago - we should continue to dig for it.

It matters, too, to quarry out any new facts there may be about the assassination of Abraham Lincoln. Or, to get away from assassination for a moment, to delve into the perceived mysteries about the catastrophe at Pearl Harbor. But the Kennedy assassination is a relatively recent event, with relevance to our time. It's not that far behind us.

One thing I have taken on board during a fairly long life is the remarkable foreshortening that comes with looking back. I now realize that half a century is actually no time at all ago, just a tiny blink. The period since 1963 has increasingly been a period during which Americans - and people in many other countries - have come to doubt the "facts" as retailed to them by their governments. There are all sorts of reasons for that faltering faith in those elected to govern, of course. It's not just the national doubt about the Kennedy assassination, but also the doubts about other events, such as Watergate and, in this last decade or so, the invasion of Iraq. The truth has not been told to the population and citizens must continue to demand it.

So, it's important for us to hold our government accountable over what happened to President Kennedy?

It's important to hold them accountable over any event that occurred in living memory - or indeed last week.

David Talbot

David Talbot has a talent for bringing the past to life. Mr. Talbot's highly acclaimed book, *Brothers: The Hidden History of the Kennedy Years*, sheds light into Robert Kennedy's immediate concerns that there was a conspiracy to murder his brother in Dallas. He spent nearly a decade interviewing former friends and co-workers of the Kennedy family to get to the bottom of that conclusion.

Mr. Talbot also raises troubling questions about what he calls the "elite" in Washington who might have enjoyed the fruits of President Kennedy's death. Who were these people, and were they involved in the murder of JFK? Who did Bobby Kennedy believe murdered his brother? Was Bobby Kennedy a "conspiracy theorist" himself?

What is your area of expertise on the Kennedy assassination?

The powers that were behind the assassination, and what Robert Kennedy was privately doing to investigate the assassination of his brother.

Can you please explain who those "powers" were, and can you also explain the dangers that President Kennedy was surrounded by in the time leading up to his death?

I think the people who organized the assassination were at the top levels of U.S. power. There's a term that's become widespread within academic and research circles in the last decade, and it's called the "deep state" or the "secret government." These are people who are usually not elected. They are very powerful figures in Wall Street, and industry, and in Washington, especially in the national security state.

These people seem to hold power from one administration to the next, and they belong to the same social clubs and organizations. They are the American elite. At the center of these power elites, I believe in terms of the Kennedy assassination, was Allen Dulles. Allen Dulles was the very definition of the power elite. He was a former Wall Street lawyer, the father of modern American intelligence, one of the founders of the CIA, and the longest serving director of the CIA under President Eisenhower, and then President Kennedy.

Of course, President Kennedy fired Dulles after the disastrous Bay of Pigs invasion. I believe what happened is that Kennedy was trying to end the Cold War, which he felt had nearly brought the world to a nuclear holocaust during the Cuban Missile crisis in 1962. He had opened up back channels of communications with Premier Khrushchev and Fidel Castro. He was trying to lead the country out of the Cold War, but just as with the war on terror, the Cold War was a massive machine that produced enormous profit for a lot of people and a lot of power for those people as well. The Cold War elite was not prepared to let that power go.

Kennedy was infringing on that power, and I believe Allen Dulles was a key member of that group who plotted against the President. I believed he used those associates of his in the national security world to green light the assassination, and I believe it also involved certain elements within the CIA that were still loyal to him. It's important to remember that Allen Dulles, in the 1950s, had built an assassination machine that was lethal throughout the world. It assassinated leaders, politicians and union activists, as well as journalists. He brought home that killing team to kill Kennedy in Dallas in 1963.

Gaeton Fonzi, the former congressional JFK researcher, believed that the murder of JFK was a message sent to the American people. Do you believe that as well?

It was a message sent and a message received, not just by the American people, but also to anyone who wanted to become President or was elected President. It was a searing message, an explosive message in broad daylight. I mean, imagine shooting the President in broad daylight, and spraying his brain matter all over his wife. You can't get anymore emphatic than that, and any more disrespectful. It was disrespectful not only to the President and our democracy, but also to his family and his wife. They had to see and experience that.

As I write about in *Brothers*, the people in that motorcade knew what happened instantly. They knew what was going on. The people in their car and the people right behind them; including Kenneth O'Donnell and Dave Powers, both White House aides to Kennedy, they were war veterans. They knew the sound of gunfire; they knew where it was coming from. They said right away it came from multiple directions, as did, of course, dozens of eyewitnesses that day in Dealey Plaza.

There was a massive cover up from the very beginning. The FBI warned Kenneth O'Donnell not to say what he truly saw, and of course he toed the party line the rest of his life. However, he did admit to Tip O'Neil, the former Speaker of the House, that he lied under pressure from the FBI when he testified to the Warren Commission that the gunfire came from behind.

A lot of people think conspiracy advocates are insane. Now, obviously there are a lot of things within the JFK assassination that are insane, such as wild theories and false witnesses, but when someone like yourself comes along, someone with experience and credibility, and you say things about a 'dark government' or 'conspiracy,' you also are written off as a conspiracy nut. So, let me ask you if you have any evidence to prove your theories true?

Yes. I have researched the subject for over six years, and I'm a journalist. Because I am a journalist and a historian, everything I write about has documentation behind it. This documentation comes from interviews I have done personally, or from government documents that have been released under the JFK Records Act.

Of course, there are wild conspiracy theories out there, and I believe that was apart of the CIA's cover up strategy as well. This part of the cover up was run by the head of counterintelligence, James Jesus Angleton. He used disinformation. He consistently flooded the public arena with lies and misleading information order to confuse and befuddle the American people until they just threw up their hands in despair, and concluded we will never know the truth.

Notice, even 52 years later, the media still says the same thing. I mean, on the 50th anniversary of the assassination the media was appalling in it's coverage of the case. This coverage is negligent, it's ignorant; it's lazy, and its cowardice. People say, "You can't keep things hidden in America." Well, you can't keep hidden who Taylor Swift is dating, but you can sure as hell keep the important stuff locked away. That's what we have learned from history.

Of course power conspires together. That's how power works. Europeans are fully aware of this; but Americans seem naive. We tend to still believe what we're taught in the class room, but older civilizations know that power kills to stay in power. Power conspires, and does terrible things.

There is the government elect, and then there are the real powers in control. We see this over and over again, yet we believe fairy tales. We tend to believe we're exceptional because we're Americans. Conspiracy simply means literally whispering among each other, and of course that happens all the time behind close doors among powerful people. And when these private conversations are occasionally revealed by some hacker, the authorities freak out. People who say all conspiracy theorists are nuts are children who want to believe in fairy tales.

You have to study these things, and be smart about each so-called conspiracy theory - and of course they are not just theories when they are documented. After doing your research, you have to make up your own mind about what is credible and what isn't. Most conspiracy theories I reject, but when you see the documentation I have about the Kennedy assassination, and study as much as I have - unlike 99.9 percent of the American media - then you come up with credible conclusions yourself.

Could you describe the CIA's tactic of disinformation during the time of President Kennedy's assassination? Do you think it continues today?

I think so. There are documents that have been released under the Freedom of Information Act, which is one of the few vestiges we have left of our democracy. One of those documents, released in the 1970s, showed that there were memos that the CIA sent to friendly reporters. These reporters included hundreds and hundreds of people all throughout the media that the CIA considered their assets. There were even some media members who were actually paid by the CIA. Some did this work as a favor to the CIA, and some saw it as their patriotic duty. But in any case, there were a lot of these helpful people in broadcasting, at the New York Times and the Washington Post, and all these people helped spread CIA disinformation. The CIA's counterintelligence department even wrote up memos for some of these "assets" that instructed people on how to rebut JFK conspiracy researchers.

A lot of people believe that Bobby Kennedy accepted the Warren Report, and rested in it. Is this true?

Well, the whole thrust of my book, *Brothers,* was to show that Bobby privately rejected both the Warren Report, and the lone gunman theory. He was caught in a terrible political dilemma once his brother was killed, and his power was immediately evaporating. The new president was his mortal enemy. They were long-time political enemies who hated one another. Lyndon Johnson wanted to isolate Bobby, to push him out right away. And the head of the FBI, J. Edgar Hoover, who was supposed to be Bobby's subordinate, also hated Bobby, and wouldn't even return his calls after his brother was killed.

The investigation of his brother's assassination was put into the hands of Kennedy enemies like Hoover and Allen Dulles, who played a key role on the Warren Commission. Allen Dulles had been fired by JFK. And yet he played a dominant role on the commission, along with former Secretary of War, John McCloy, who was forced out of the Kennedy administration because as the head of arms control he was getting nowhere in negotiations with Russia.

The other problem that Bobby Kennedy had was that if he went public it would cause mass chaos in our country. This observation at the time was made by the very astute writer, M.S. Arnoni, publisher of an independent journal called Minority of One. He wrote an article in January 1964, as the Warren Commission was beginning, and said if a public figure like Bobby Kennedy were to speak out about the truth, you could have a civil crisis in the country. You could have one faction of the American military firing at another, and there would be blood in the streets. There was trauma among the American people over the assassination, and for the President's brother to come out and say that he believed certain forces in the U.S. government were responsible for it would have provoked an enormous crisis.

So, Bobby chose to bide his time, and he felt he couldn't do anything until he was the President himself. In 1968, after much deliberation, he decided he would run for that office. Here is a guy with 10 or 11 children. He was responsible for so much life. He also had many members of his family, including Ted Kennedy and Jacqueline Kennedy, begging him not to run, knowing how dangerous it would for him to run. But he decided he had to run, not just to bring the Vietnam War to a close, and to heal the racial strife within our country, but also to finally resolve his brother's case, which had been covered up ever since the day it happened.

And so he decided to run in 1968, and he was privately telling people that he was going to reopen the investigation of his brother's murder. He was trying to find out as much as he could about that. He was already using surrogates such as Walter Sheridan, a former FBI investigator, who was his top investigator. He was asking him to secretly follow every lead he could. He also asked his press secretary Frank Mankiewicz to read all that he could, including all the conspiracy literature, so he would be up to date when Bobby wanted to reopen the investigation. He was getting his ducks in a row, and was preparing to do reopen the case, when he himself was murdered after winning the California primary in 1968.

Who were the main suspects that Bobby investigated?

We know from the first minutes and hours after Dallas where Bobby's suspicions go, based on the phone calls he made, and the conversations he was having from his home in Virginia. He went into a frenzy trying to figure this out as quickly as he could. And because Bobby was the Attorney General, and a long time organized crime crusader, as well as someone who was overseeing the CIA for his brother, he had lots of knowledge about the darker corners of American power, so he knew right away where to look.

His suspicions immediately went to the CIA and the CIA's operations against Castro. Those covert operations – which included assassination plots against Castro that were not authorized by President Kennedy - were based in part on an alliance with the Mafia. President Eisenhower and Allen Dulles had initiated this plan involving the mafia to kill

Castro back in 1960, before JFK was elected, and that operation continued without Kennedy's knowledge. It was covered up, and they lied to Bobby about it because Bobby was the former Chief Counsel of the Senate rackets committee and personally loathed the Mafia. And so, when he was told about this contract with Mafia by the CIA in 1962, he flipped out.

The CIA assured him that these plans had been stopped, but they hadn't. The two contacts the CIA used to work with the Mafia were Robert Maheu, who was the head of a major private intelligence firm and was used as a CIA contractor, and William Harvey, who was the head of the CIA assassinations unit. Those were the two key guys who oversaw the CIA's relationship with the Mafia, and I think Harvey was also involved in Dallas.

In your book, "Brothers," you make it a point that there is a darker history to the cold war. Can you please explain what you mean by that, and how that darker side may have played a role in the Kennedy assassination?

In the cold war, we barely avoided a nuclear confrontation. We now know we came close to using nuclear weapons in several occasions. John Foster Dulles, who was Allen Dulles's brother, was Secretary of State under Eisenhower and wanted to use nuclear weapons against the Vietnamese when the French started to lose their colonial war against them. That's just one example of how these Cold War warriors thought.

However, the main way the Cold War was enforced by the United States was through clandestine methods. The CIA was at the forefront of that. Some of this has been well documented by congressional committees and historians. There are such things as the overthrow of the government in the Congo, the Arbenz government in Guatemala, and the Mosaddeq government in Iran. In both those last two cases, Guatemala and Iran, when the CIA overthrew those democratically elected governments, accusing them of being communists, which was a lie and a cover, it led to decades of hatred and animosity towards our people.

Those are only the things that were documented. There were other things all over the world the CIA committed, yet were never revealed. We kidnapped people, and tortured them. Dulles and the CIA did this in the 1950s. There was a professor at Columbia University. He was an outspoken critic of a dictator in the Dominican Republic, Trujillo, and he had inside information about this government because he had previously worked inside it. But Trujillo was a staunch U.S. ally. So, the CIA had this professor kidnapped in New York City and flown by a private airplane to the Dominican Republic where he was tortured and eventually murdered.

This is what happens when you have intelligence agencies with no or little oversight. When Congress is asleep at the wheel, and the American people are apathetic, people look the other way. America needs to cleanse its soul, and reckon with its history. Kennedy stood up to these powers and told them *"No,"* and he paid the ultimate price for it.

How does the Cuban exile community fit into your picture of the JFK assassination?

Members of that community were utilized by the CIA, obviously to try and overthrow Castro, and I think there may also have been some of these Cuban militants involved in Dallas. There was a kind of merger, at the time, between lower level CIA hit men, and Cuban exiles, and their Mafia counterparts. They worked together, in places like the JM/WAVE station in Miami, which was the largest CIA station in the world. The Cuban exiles certainly weren't the brains behind the assassination, but some were probably useful tools.

Who is Lee Harvey Oswald to you?

I think Lee Oswald was the classic victim type. He had no father. He had an emotionally volatile mother. He came from difficult circumstances, poor, going from one home to the next while moving around the country. He was eager to move away from that situation. He was a bright young man, not stupid like some may think. He was self-taught, yet probably dyslexic. He spent a lot of time at the library, probably having a hard time reading, but he wanted to make something better of himself.

He was intrigued by the undercover world of FBI agents and that sort of thing. Eventually, he followed his two older brothers into the military to get away from his mother. He went to the Marines of course. He ended up at a base in Japan, Atsugi air base, which was a base that housed the U2 spy plane; it was a CIA connected base. He probably came to the attention of some intelligence authorities at that point in time.

He had aspirations to see the world. He was curious about the Soviet

Union. I think he genuinely had left wing ideals. It seems as if military and intelligence authorities were aware of that. They saw him as someone they could use as a false defector, or perhaps exploit his genuine interest in visiting the Soviet Union.

I don't think he had the full training of an intelligence agent himself. But he put himself in the position of being used by intelligence officials. I think that that odd relationship between Oswald and American intelligence, particularly the CIA, began as early as Japan. We certainly know they were tracking him while he was in the Soviet Union, and when he came back to the U.S. with a Russian wife, he was miraculously waved back into the country -- even after renouncing his citizenship and threatening to reveal classified information he acquired at Atsugi.

That's a really strange thing if you think about it. Imagine something like that happening in the height of the Cold War - or even today, you know, with the war on terror. What if you went overseas and joined Al Qaeda and bitterly denounced America, and then came home with an Islamic wife, and you were not stopped at the border and you were not questioned by law enforcement? Wouldn't observers think that was very, very strange? But that's what happened with Oswald. He comes home unmolested by authorities and takes up residence with his family in Texas, under the benign supervision of a CIA connected, globe-trotting businessman named George de Mohrenschildt.

I think Lee Harvey Oswald, as Senator Schweiker from Pennsylvania has previously stated, had the "fingerprints of intelligence" all over him. I think he was being manipulated by intelligence agencies, being sent here and there, and a profile and image was being created around him; one that presented him as a dangerous and radical leftist.

I think he was set up to take the blame for the assassination of President Kennedy. I think, after the assassination, he was a smart enough guy to figure out how he was being set up, which is why he yelled, "I'm a patsy!"

There is also interesting research that has been done about the post-assassination phone calls he made. While he was in custody he tried to call someone in Raleigh, North Carolina. Some people have speculated, including Victor Marchetti, who was a former CIA official that this phone call was to his intelligence cut out, and he was trying to reach out to his intelligence contacts to tell them he was in trouble. It was basically an S.O.S. call. Intelligence did not want to speak with him, and I think they feared he would eventually start to talk, which would lead to his connections with them. So they had to get rid of him, which is where Jack Ruby stepped in.

So what about the Mafia? How do they tie into this intelligence theory?

Well, as I said, the Mafia had been working closely with the CIA since the anti-Castro operations, and there were also ties between American intelligence and the Mafia going all the way back to World War II. More currently, they were tied together by their efforts to kill Castro. They were well aware of each other and worked together.

People like William Harvey of the CIA worked side by side with Mafia don Johnny Roselli, who was the diplomat for the Mafia. So, that machinery was already in place. But, I don't think the Mafia organized the assassination of President Kennedy, or the cover up either. They didn't have the power to do that, and if it were only them involved, Robert Kennedy would have come down on them with a sledgehammer, because that is who he was. No other Attorney General had prosecuted more members of the Mafia than he had. So, obviously it wasn't just the Mafia. They were a partner, but only a junior partner within the assassination operation.

Now, the key role of the Mafia was the Jack Ruby hit on Oswald. The Mafia had Ruby by the throat. He had to do what they told him to do. They told him he would be a hero if he killed Oswald, and that he would get out of jail soon after. Robert Kennedy, after the assassination, immediately investigated Ruby. His investigators told him that Ruby was mobbed up, and connected to the Mafia in Chicago and Dallas. And as Frank Mankiewicz, Bobby's press aide, later told me, when Bobby sought the phone records of people who Jack Ruby was talking with before he shot Oswald, it read just like the witness list of the Mafia figures whom Bobby had subpoenaed before the rackets committee back in the 1950s. So, Bobby was aware of how connected Ruby was to organized crime.

And of course, later the fairytale was put out that Ruby had felt overcome with emotion over President Kennedy's death, and he wanted to protect Jackie Kennedy from having to come to Dallas and testify in a trial, so he eliminated Oswald; which of course is a fairytale.

Lone nut advocates claim that Oswald was not set up at all. They see Oswald as a violent and sociopathic narcissist who craved political power and fame. They also claim the Walker shooting proves that Oswald was a murderous nut. What do you counter those charges with?

Well, I think more investigation needs to be done on the Walker shooting. That's still murky, and I don't think Oswald definitely can be named the gunman that night. If he was involved, there seems to be another person in a car there that night. So, that actually merits further investigation.

But, despite Oswald's character, what was his motive in killing President Kennedy? The Warren Commission never could come up with a solid one, and they basically threw up their hands over it. The best they could do is to speculate that Oswald was envious of Kennedy, and hated any authority because he himself was a loser. They just speculated that he wanted to bring down this glamorous and wealthy President out of his own frustration and bitterness.

But that didn't really add up, because everyone who was close to Oswald, including Ruth and Michael Paine, who took Marina in when she and Lee separated, said that Oswald actually liked the President. George de Mohrenschildt, Oswald's CIA babysitter, said that Lee actually had great respect for President Kennedy. He said Oswald admired the President's position on civil rights, and he thought he was a young and dynamic man, and was a great force for change in the country.

Like I previously stated, I think Oswald was a guy who leaned towards the left. So, if anything, he admired Kennedy as a liberal president. I mean, how do you have Oswald shooting this right-wing, John Bircher (General Edwin Walker) and then turning around and killing this liberal president? I think the motives that the lone nut camp brings up are always murky, and based on speculation. That, to me, is one of the weakest parts of their arguments. When you read the Warren Commission proceedings, and the discussions the staff was having, they're completely baffled as to why Oswald would have killed Kennedy.

If you could sum it up, what happened on November 22, 1963?

I think Oswald was used as a fall guy. And, as a side note, the last investigation that was ever carried out by the government into the Kennedy assassination found that there was evidence for a conspiracy. So, the last official word about the assassination was that, yes, there was a conspiracy. The American people should know about that, and should know more about the work done by Gaeton Fonzi, who was a key investigator for the House Select Committee on Assassinations, and the author of *The Last Investigation*.

That Committee came close to the truth, and they didn't get there because of the huge political pressure put on them to wrap things up. They dug up a lot of important information for future researchers and historians. In any case, that committee found that Oswald had unnamed co-conspirators with him in the plot – although I'm not certain he was involved at all. I think his main role was to play the part of the useful culprit.

I think President Kennedy was caught in a cross fire in Dealey Plaza, and that his actual killers were professional snipers who were very effective that day. I think the fatal shot came from the grassy knoll, blowing out the back of JFK's head. The Zapruder film shows this when Kennedy is thrown violently backwards as if he was hit from the front. Lone nut advocates have tried all kinds of different ways to explain this away. They come up with all sorts of unusual interpretations of the law of physics - even if it defies all human eyesight and reason.

But, all you have to do is keep your eyes open, watch the Zapruder film, and see how his head kicks back, and I think it will be obvious. I think this sniper team was managed by the CIA - whose assassination unit had been targeting heads of states and other political enemies for years. And by the way, the murder of JFK was very similar to another assassination attempt around that time period. There was an attempt on the President of France, Charles de Gaulle, in his motorcade in Paris. He too was also the victim of a sniper attack. He believed the CIA was responsible for this as well, because he had been defying U.S. policy in various ways.

That is an interesting footnote in history. Throughout the early 60s, there were attempts to overthrow De Gaulle and kill him. Kennedy helped stop one such coup attempt around the time of the Bay of Pigs in 1961 - a plot that had the backing of the CIA. De Gaulle lived, while Kennedy didn't, because the French leader had a more loyal and trustworthy presidential security detail than JFK did. So the CIA was very experienced at these things, and President Kennedy was the victim of a professional hit.

Lee Harvey Oswald was set up. He was a terrible marksman, and we know this from his time in the Marines, and also his time in Russia. Oswald's friends in Russia, when later interviewed, claimed that Oswald would go out on hunting trips with them, and he was such a bad shot when they were trying to shoot rabbits that they would pity him and shoot a rabbit themselves in order to give it to him. So, we're supposed to believe that this poor marksmen, using a faulty sighted, old World War II, bolt action rifle, pulled off the marksman's feat of the century by firing in rapid succession at a moving target? That defies all logic, and it's really an insult to the American people's intelligence.

As you look in detail at what the Warren Report was actually saying, such as how the magic bullet did so much damage, and then came out virtually unscathed, all of this is absurd. It defies all logic. And also, the testimony of the surgeons in Dallas, who labored over the dying President at Parkland Memorial Hospital, raises grave doubts about the official story. Years later, members of that medical team, when they felt it was safe to do so, began telling the truth, and they said that there was clear evidence that Kennedy was shot from the front, and not just from behind. To their credit, two of these surgeons came forward and told what they saw.

You just have to keep your eyes open, and study the case, and the truth is out there. I mean, I'm glad that you, as a younger person, have taken an interest. I say that because this case is not just dead history. This is live history, and it's something that continues to weigh heavy on the American people, because if you can't solve a mystery like this, then you can't protect your own democracy. So, going back to that day, unless we get to the bottom of this case, we really have no control over the truth that our government sells us. If we have no control of our past, then we have no control over our future.

What advice would you give future researchers in their search for the truth?

Here's my advice not just for researchers, but for the country as well. I think we need a public inquiry. Back in the Vietnam War days, Bertrand Russell, the great British philosopher, convened a citizen's commission to analyze the Vietnam War, and the war crimes that were being committed there. There were a number of experts, and leading authorities who were called to testify before that commission, and it got a lot of publicity. This raised public awareness about the U.S. government's genocidal policies in Southeast Asia - and this is what we need today to get to the bottom of other unresolved traumas in our history.

I don't think politically, given what Congress is like these days, that we will get a congressional committee to reopen the Kennedy investigation. And, by the way, we also need to reopen the inquiries into the murders of Robert Kennedy and Martin Luther King, Jr. I believe there was open war on liberal and left-wing and radical leaders in this country during the 1960s - and these assassinations changed the course of U.S. history in a profoundly tragic way for the country. So, we need an independent commission that would include a number of legal experts that could hear testimony from the great number of researchers who have been collecting information, and also from the few witnesses who are still alive. Then, if there's enough public pressure, perhaps congress will finally use its power to solve these cases. And they can begin by forcing the CIA to follow the law- The JFK Records Act – and release all the public documents it is illegally withholding from the American people.

We will not grow as a country until we can move forward on this. Do the Americans want the truth at long last? I hope they do, while it can still make a difference. Our democracy can't survive the reign of secrecy and lies.

David Scheim

David Scheim has a doctorate in Mathematics. He also is a master of solving many of the problems found in the Kennedy assassination. Mr. Scheim spent a decade of his life researching this case. His book, *Contract on America: The Mafia Murder of President John F. Kennedy* details the history of Lee Harvey Oswald's murderer, Jack Ruby, and provides a detailed account of possible Mafia involvement in a conspiracy to murder the president. I wanted the reader to get this side of the case because it is intriguing, if not persuasive.

The Mafia hated President Kennedy, and his brother Robert for their war on their illegal operations in the United States. Did this hatred lead the Mafia to take on one of the most daring hits of the century?

What is your area of expertise in the JFK assassination?

I came into this really with no background at all; I was just interested in it. My background is I have a Ph.D. in math and worked in medical informatics at NIH, so I really had no particular background; I just spent ten years studying the case very closely.

Since your primary studies in the case involve the Mafia, who was Jack Ruby?

Jack Ruby was someone growing up in prohibition, very poor, in the Chicago ghetto. His story is not a particularly distinguished story; he just fell in with racketeers at a very young age. Ruby started out in Chicago as a minor level hoodlum. At a certain point, after a decade or so of this, a Chicago group went down to Dallas to take over the rackets there, and Ruby was one of those that came down with the group, and after a few decades in Dallas, most of those people either died or were killed and he was one of those few pioneers left. And so, he ended up as someone who had some degree of stature with the mob in Dallas. For example, he was a frequent visitor of Joseph Civello, who was the Mafia boss of Dallas. This is who Jack Ruby was, and it's all documented; a lot of this stuff about his life is in FBI reports.

Could you describe Jack Ruby's ties to organized crime?

Well, we have a lot of bits and pieces of information. We know he was involved in gambling operations, and another report has him working in one of the slot machine warehouses. Basically, gambling was a mob controlled operation, so anyone who was at a management level, like Ruby, was hooked in with the mob. So, Jack Ruby is running gambling operations.

There is an FBI report dated a few or so years before the assassination in which a narcotics informant describes Jack Ruby as being one of the leaders of a narcotics operation operating between Texas and Mexico. So, we have bits and pieces of his connections.

His activities seem to include gambling, narcotics, police corruption, a bit of prostitution, and his contacts are at a very high level with people like Joseph Civello of Dallas, and Joseph Campisi, the Mafia under-boss who was one of the first people to visit Ruby in jail after he shot Oswald. Then we have the phone records that link him to mobsters all over the country. This wasn't just routine business. I don't think we have a complete picture, but we do have many important fragments.

Some researchers claim that after Ruby had shot Oswald, and was visited by the Mafia under-boss Joseph Campisi, it actually shows the Mafia had nothing to do with it because that would be out of character for the Mafia, and wouldn't be a smart move. What do you think of that?

Yeah, I mean that's a really bright statement. That maybe Ruby wouldn't have called all of these people or wouldn't have spoken to anybody connected to the mob if they were involved in the assassination. I mean, that would assume perfect wisdom from the mob, where they know this will go into history. It's an assumption that everything might go perfectly instead of the mob having to react to some emergency situation where Ruby might say something he shouldn't that would bring them down. This is to assume an all-wise Joseph Campisi. I really think that's a weak argument. It's like saying that that a killer wouldn't have committed a murder if he was going to leave his fingerprints there. I mean, that statement makes no sense.

Why did the Warren Commission not pursue a stronger interrogation of Jack Ruby?

Yeah, this is a question I was asked in a lot of news and radio interviews. At the beginning, I really could only speculate, and then a few years after my book came out I got to meet with Judge Burt Griffin for three hours. I was in Dealey plaza and got the whole story. Griffin was the only person who worked for the Warren Commission to investigate Jack Ruby. He had a partner, but the partner got sick, so Griffin pretty much did all of the research on his own.

Griffin told me the Warren Commission was initially given six months to come up with its report; they were working under that kind of pressure. So, there was an assassination conference in D.C. at the end of September, where Robert Blakey spoke and explained how when you're given a timeline for a final report, you have to start writing the report months and months before the report is due. You can't just think, 'okay, I was given six months to investigate,' because you don't have six months to investigate. A six-month deadline means you have a few weeks to investigate it, and five months to write the report, because writing a report is a pretty onerous thing, and has to be cleared by a lot of people. So, essentially they (the Warren Commission) were working under a timeline that allowed no opportunity to do just about anything other than what Hoover had already decided to do. So, he felt like this environment didn't allow any kind of investigation at all.

Then, his deadline was extended and you can see Burt Griffin's suspicions about Jack Ruby rising. So, he was suspicious. But, in the end, he was operating as one person. He had the CIA stonewalling him, and a rushed deadline to meet, so there was a lot of information he never got to see. He felt that if he couldn't prove Ruby was a part of a conspiracy, he was obliged to write the report they wanted him to write. That's what he said.

If the Mafia was involved in the murder of President Kennedy, what kind of motive did they have to commit such a crime?

Basically, the Mafia was on the verge of being wiped out under Robert Kennedy. He was the attorney general under JFK, and had worked for the Senate McClellan Committee, who went after labor racketeering. So, under JFK, the Mafia was being pressed against the wall. There were thousands of Mafia figures either indicted or convicted or under such tight surveillance that they could barely operate.

This was happening up through mid-1963, but that was just a warm up because Robert Kennedy and the Joseph Valachi hearings occurred in the fall of 1963, in which Robert Kennedy was indicating that this was going to be a preview of a whole higher level of prosecution for the Mafia.

Also, the Mafia had a key base of operations in Cuba. They were involved in gambling, narcotics and money laundering there, and when Castro rose to power these financial sources were all threatened. Ultimately the Mafia's casinos were shut down, and they were furious. They wanted Castro dead, and supported anti-Castro Cubans. Now, when Kennedy refused to provide air support at the Bay of Pigs, one Mafia-connected member is alleged to say, *"Kennedy just signed his death warrant."*

People claim, historically speaking, that the Mafia didn't have the means or power to pull off a Presidential assassination. What do you make of that assessment?

I never said *only* the Mafia was involved in the Kennedy assassination. What I tried to do was to stick to, as carefully as I could, the hard evidence. I think when I wrote my book I didn't feel there was persuasive evidence for anyone to be involved but the Mafia. But, I think at this point there's some pretty good evidence of the Mafia's collaborators being involved. Again, as I wrote the book, I never said the Mafia was the driver; all I said is when we look at what happened, there is one person who we know is involved, and that is Jack Ruby.

Oswald, for all we know, could have been a patsy. There are a lot of questions as to whether Oswald was a shooter, or someone who was set up. So, we do not have any definitive evidence as to who Oswald was. But, there's no question as to who Jack Ruby was. He's the only person who we can conclusively link to the case, and Ruby is a mob guy. So, I think it's a conservative position to say this is where we start. Other than that, I have no idea where the Mafia is at in the pecking order.

Are there any ties with Oswald and Organized Crime?

Yeah, David Ferrie and, his uncle, Dutz Murrett.

Now that we have evidence that the CIA has deceived the American people concerning the JFK files they have withheld, is it your opinion that lower level CIA members possibly worked with the Mafia to murder the President?

Absolutely. I mean, if someone were to just ask me what I think, my impression is that it's absolutely possible. G. Robert Blakey really blasted the CIA for obstructing the investigation of the HSCA (House Select Committee on Assassinations). Whoever Oswald was, it was significant that although he portrayed himself as pro-Castro, he actually had contacts with an anti-Castro group. This connection was something the House Select Committee wanted to know more about. So, they had these two staffers working under Blakey who really pushed this point. They were allowed to work at CIA headquarters and push for documents, but at a certain point that got shut down.

Ultimately, they were interested in knowing who the CIA handler was for this anti-Castro group that Oswald had contact with in New Orleans. They asked George Joannides, the liaison between the CIA and the HSCA, if he knew of any documents that could show who this handler was, and he said he checked and didn't find anything about that handler. The punch line is that Joannides himself was this guy who was the CIA handler Blakey was looking for, so that was an outright lie on something that was important.

G. Robert Blakey essentially said that obstructing a congressional investigation, in some sense, is almost an act that's in character with killing the President. It's fairly subversive activity against our democracy, and this struck me as very important.

Do you think the Mafia and the CIA turned their plots to kill Castro around on Kennedy?

I think the Mafia and the CIA were in the habit of working with each other and when they both came to hate Kennedy they may have become a part of the coalition to kill Kennedy.

Lone nut advocates love to use Jack Ruby's character as proof for their position on the case. They say his narcissistic craving led him to kill Oswald, because ultimately he wanted to be a hero. Does Ruby's character discount him from being used in a conspiracy to you?

The poster boy for this characterization of Ruby is a man named Tony Zoppi.

It's interesting to note that when you have a theory, it's important to find out who is one of the prominent people that disagree with your theory so you can see their argument as well. Gerald Posner sort of filled that role to a degree. His book, *Case Closed*, got fairly wide praise, and he based his case on Ruby being this kind of loner person through Tony Zoppi. Zoppi is one of the key people where Posner pulls his assessment of Ruby from.

Zoppi says that Ruby is a nobody, and just wanted attention. But, it turns out that Zoppi is someone who was close with Joseph Campisi. He's a guy who is up to his ears in questionable ties with the Mafia. Zoppi said he saw Ruby the morning of the assassination. Ruby's activities that morning were suspicious and so were his pre-assassination moves as well. I mean, the day before the assassination, the Secret Service produced a report saying Ruby was seen by three witnesses a few blocks from the president's hotel in Houston. So, there was a lot of suspicious activity in regards to Ruby's movements in all the days surrounding the assassination.

And, there's a whole series of contradictory alibi's for that time period, and one them came from Tony Zoppi. He fills out Ruby's alibi for the morning of the assassination. Zoppi said Ruby came to see him, and tells that to the Warren Commission, but Posner says he knows that's not true; that Zoppi admitted to him that he was lying. So, here's a guy who commits what's equivalent to perjury on a very key part of the assassination. This is guy who has routine mob contacts, and this is the guy who Posner puts forward as the poster boy of the "*loner Ruby*" point of view.

I mean, I really think this is all a joke. It just blows in the face of all the evidence, and if you're willing to believe Zoppi against dozens of FBI files, go ahead.

What did Jack Ruby have to say after the assassination?

He requested repeatedly to testify before the Warren Commission, they initially refused, but he pressed and pressed and eventually got that opportunity. Then he presses and presses afterwards to have a polygraph hearing, and sort of the point of his story was that he wanted to prove to the American people that he did this out of patriotism. And so, that's what he said his motive was, but it's obvious he's not telling the truth, and that he's calculated in getting stuff into the records.

It's interesting that when he goes before the Warren Commission, he starts doing this story about Jackie Kennedy, and then he jokes around about his testimony with a Secret Service member, like it's a script. So, between his testimony to the Warren Commission, and his polygraph hearing, he says "Here's a guy who didn't even vote, how come he gets so patriotically involved?"

Do you believe Ruby's "patriotic testimony?"

Ruby himself mocks that story. He totally rips it to shreds in his own testimony. It doesn't line up with the evidence either. The narcotics operations and gambling operations; the phone calls and visits to Joseph Civello; I mean, this shows that's not who Ruby is according to historical facts. That *"lone patriot"* theory is according to Zoppi. Both sides of Ruby cannot be true. They're contradictory; they can't both be true. And the other is that this idea that Ruby did it out of patriotism is a joke, and Ruby points that out himself.

People say it was impossible that there was a conspiracy, because Ruby was lucky to get to the county jail before they had transferred Oswald. Oswald was scheduled to be transferred after 10 A.M., and they say the reason he was delayed from that deadline was because the postal inspector, Harry Holmes, came down out of mere chance. Do you think this point is a hole in the conspiracy theory?

Right, and that's the most substantive question along those lines.

Ruby shot Oswald at 11:21 A.M., almost five minutes after he left the Western Union office, where he wired funds to Karen Carlin. In light of that, how would he have known if he might see Oswald in enough time to kill him?

The simple answer to that is that it's very clear that this telegram was staged precisely to establish an alibi for the killing. I mean, here's a guy who drove a hundred miles an hour, who didn't pay his tickets, who's close to the police, constantly serving them drinks, and committing crimes right under their eyes. So, it terms of petty stuff, this is not a guy who would go down to the Western Union office if she really did need the money. To make this story sound credible they decided to set something up, because no one was going to believe she just needed this money out of the blue, and then Ruby just went down there to wire the money to her. So, they said, "Let's set up a story that she came down the night before to a garage, and there was this conversation about her needing money." They tried to make this look a certain way.

But, when you look at all the witnesses' stories involved in this, it's sort of like a keystone cops comedy routine. They are all completely different. You know, she supposedly drove there, and then she says she took the bus, and the stories just wildly contradict each other. You don't have a germ of consistency in these stories. The idea is that Ruby got this call at home that she needed money. But, the time he was supposed to be taking this call, he's seen by three newsmen pacing around downtown in front of their cameras. He's standing there waiting for at least an hour, and all three identify him.

The cleaning lady calls his apartment and speaks to someone, but the person she speaks to has no idea of the cleaning arrangements, and she says Ruby doesn't sound like himself. This corroborates the fact that he was seen by the newsman. So, yeah, Ruby gets a signal to go to the Western Union office, does his thing, and then shows up.

I think it's important to understand that gambling doesn't go on without police collusion. So, he could have colluded with someone in the police force that he had previously worked with in other shady dealings. I mean, there are many examples of him doing that throughout his personal life.

Why would the Mafia leave Ruby alive to talk after he killed Oswald?

Ruby shoots Oswald, which is really suspicious and the Europeans immediately think it's a conspiracy. If someone shoots Ruby after that it's just a little too much, so they can't do that.

What members of Organized Crime do you believe were involved in the assassination?

Carlos Marcello, Santos Trafficante and Jimmy Hoffa are key suspects in this case. All of them, around the summer of 1962 and on, were credibly reported to have plotted the deaths of John Kennedy and Robert Kennedy. John Kennedy's threats were from Trafficante and Marcello, and Robert Kennedy's were from Jimmy Hoffa. In Hoffa's case it may well be that he was ultimately convinced of the logic that if they killed Robert Kennedy, John Kennedy would just wipe them all out, and do a real investigation on them. Robert Kennedy's power ultimately resided with the president. So, it seems as if Hoffa's scenario of shooting Robert Kennedy in a convertible, with a high powered rifle could have been easily switched to a plot against John Kennedy. Also, when you look at Ruby's phone calls, many of these callers from Organized Crime are linked with these three people.

What happened on November 22, 1963 in Dallas Texas?

I think if you asked one of the plotters who were there, or one of the organizers, I think it was very complicated. I don't think any of them knew it all, or could give a straight answer to that question. All I would say is that a lot of people had come to hate Kennedy. He was moving forward very quickly, and many considered him radical.

I think that America, at Kennedy's time, was heading towards a permanent state of war. What bothered Kennedy about this scenario was the nuclear threat, so he made certain moves to wind down the arms race and some saw this as traitorous. This is just a hunch, but I feel like some within CIA circles may have felt at the time that all of the moves that Kennedy was making were treasonous, and maybe 20 years later they had a change of heart about him; I don't know. I mean, in Kennedy's case, obviously he was a brilliant and good hearted person, but I think there was a circle within the establishment that felt like he was a traitor and that he had to go.

That's what I would say. I think that a lot of forces came together to plot this, and we don't know the details of that plot. But, we do know it was a conspiracy, and we know one person, Jack Ruby, who was a mobster, that showed the hand of the mob in that conspiracy. That's the one piece of solidity we can hang onto in this case.

Robert McClelland

There is a lot of mystery surrounding the medical evidence in the Kennedy assassination. Was President Kennedy shot from the front or from behind? Did he have an exit wound in the back of his head, or was that just an honest mistake on behalf of those who thought they saw such a wound? What about the president's autopsy photos? Did they show the same wounds that the Dallas doctors saw when they worked on JFK? All of these questions usually raise more questions, but some of them can be resolved with this interview.

I want to introduce you to Dr. Robert McClelland. He was one of the trauma room surgeons who worked on President Kennedy at Parkland Hospital on November 22, 1963. When I spoke with Dr. McClelland, I could hear the conviction in his voice about his surety of what he experienced in Dallas. His memory is sharp and very detailed. His testimony is vital when it comes to understanding the medical aspects of this case. Let's step into history.

How are you connected to President Kennedy's assassination?

Well, I was involved as one of the doctors at Parkland Hospital, who was first called to treat the president when he was brought into the Parkland Hospital emergency room. That was how I entered the story.

Could you describe what is was like that day?

It was about noon that day. I was at Parkland Hospital, and I was in a conference room showing an instructional movie to some of the senior surgery residents. And so, that was kind of a routine thing we did and while I was in midst of that, I heard a knock on the door of the conference room where I was and I looked out. Standing there was Dr. Charles Crenshaw, who was one of our senior surgery residents and he said, "Doctor, can you step outside for a moment? I need to tell you something."

So, I said, "Sure."

I shut off the movie projector and stepped out again and Dr. Crenshaw said they had just called the emergency room from the police station downtown saying they were bringing President Kennedy to the emergency room because he had been shot during his motorcade downtown, and they wanted all the faculty surgeons to come down to emergency room at Parkland right away.

So, that's how I first heard about it, and where I was.

After this, Dr. Crenshaw and I got onto the elevator at Parkland and rode two floors down to the emergency room. On the way down, we were talking with one another, trying to cheer ourselves up I suppose, and speculating that many times we get things into the emergency room that are said to be bad, but when we get there it's not that bad. So we were hoping that was the case.

Then the elevator came open and we went to the emergency room. Dr. Crenshaw and I stepped out into an area called "The Pit." This was the central part of the emergency room at Parkland, and I saw something there I had never seen before, which astonished me, and that was the whole area, which was 50 feet on one side and 50 feet on another, packed with men standing shoulder to shoulder with business suits and hats. And, I never had seen anything like that.

So as I took that in, that crowd of people parted and made a sort of natural corridor through the emergency room pit, down to the hallway off of the pit, which had two emergency rooms on each side. There was Operating Room One through Two on the right side and Operating Room Three through Four on the left side, and when that corridor opened up, it made it possible for me to see into the hallway outside of those four operating rooms. Sitting on a folding chair outside of Operating Room One was Mrs. Kennedy in her bloody clothing.

So, I thought to myself, *this is as bad as they said it was.*

I had to literally force myself to keep walking down toward her and Trauma Room One. Standing outside those rooms was Mrs. Doris Nelson, who was the nurse in charge at the emergency room. She was standing between two secret service men, telling them who to let go by into the trauma room. They motioned me on through and I walked by Mrs. Kennedy, pushed the door open, walked in and I was immediately confronted by the terrible sight of the president lying on his back on an emergency room cart, with an emergency light shining down on his bloody head.

I looked around, and was glad I was not alone when I saw my associates Dr. Perry and Dr. Baxter, who were on the surgery faculty with me and had just received entry into the room. I saw where they were and I went and stood at the head of the cart where the president was lying. It was obvious to me that he had a fatal wound, when I stood there because the whole back part of the right side of his head and the brain was gone, and that was a mortal wound.

When he arrived at the hospital he was still making attempts to breathe and had some cardiac activity when he was brought in, and even there in the trauma room he still had some electric cartographic activity, but wasn't attempting to breathe anymore, so it was probably within three or four minutes after he came into Trauma Room One that he was announced dead by Dr. Clark, who was our neurosurgery professor and had come into the room.

When that happened, there had been a huge number of people who had come into the trauma room and they began to leave, and as they were leaving, they pushed the cart that the President was lying on toward the wall; Dr. Baxter and I got trapped between the cart and the wall. We had to stand there while everyone left the room and when they finally emptied out we began to push the cart out of the way so we could walk around it.

But before we could do that, the door to Trauma Room One pushed open again and a priest came in, which we later learned was Father Hubert. So, in order to get out of the room we would have had to push him out of the way, so he and I just froze again where we were, and found ourselves having to witness the President's last rites. And what Father Hubert did, he came over to head of where the President was lying, his face had been covered with a sheet, and Father Hubert pushed the sheet back and leaned over President Kennedy, and all I could hear him say was the first phrase "If thou livest..." but I couldn't hear anything else he said and he went ahead and administered the last rites.

Just as he finished that, the door to Trauma Room One came open again and Mrs. Kennedy walked in and stood across from Dr. Baxter and I, who were at the front of the cart. And I couldn't hear what she said because she spoke in such a quiet voice, but she asked Father Hubert apparently, in the context of how he answered her, if the president had received the last rites.

Father Hubert answered, "Yes, I've given him conditional absolution."

At the word "conditional" Mrs. Kennedy grimaced a bit, but she didn't say anything and she stood there for a moment and made a ring exchange from her finger to his finger, and from his finger to hers and I can't describe it more forward than that. She stood there for a few moments and then she went to the foot of the cart where the President's bare right foot was protruding out of the sheet and she stood there by his foot for a moment, then leaned over and kissed his foot, and turned and walked out of the room.

That was the last we saw of her that day, or ever. After that, we went back upstairs, sat around, and went over what happened with Dr. Perry and some of our other associates. That's how it happened with my involvement at Parkland that day.

I have a question about the head wound you saw on President Kennedy. I want to ask you this question in detail, because some say that you're mistaken in the way you just described the wound in the back of his head. Some claim because you didn't turn the President around, you might be mistaken, because they claim there was never a wound in the back of President Kennedy's head. Could you describe what you said in detail or tell us if you ever looked behind his head to confirm a wound in the back of his head?

Well, that's not quite true. I was standing at the back of the head; I was standing about 18 inches above the back of his head, so I was looking directly down into a wound in the back of his head that was probably five or six inches in diameter. It included most of the right part of the back of his head and a little bit of the back part of the top of his head. It was a massive wound, and all of the brain of that part of his head had been blown out. So, I got a very long look at that directly over a period of five or six minutes while Dr. Perry and Dr. Baxter were exploring the neck and putting in a tracheotomy line.

I just stood there and looked down into that wound, so I wasn't diverted from anything else. I just looked into that wound for around three or four minutes before he was pronounced dead, so I have a very vivid impression of what the wound looked like in the back of his head.

So, you have no doubt in your mind that there was a wound in the right rear portion of President Kennedy's head?

Oh gosh, no more so than the sun comes up every morning. I saw that directly as I said from a distance of maybe 18 inches above it, and stared at that wound for five or six minutes before he was pronounced dead.

Did the other doctors see the same thing?

No. They weren't in the position I was in. Dr. Perry and Dr. Baxter were working on the president's neck, doing the tracheotomy. So, they turned all their attention towards that, not the wound at his head. And, people who were walking around the trauma room didn't get anything but indirect glances at the head. I had the best and most direct view for the longest period.

Now, I want to ask you about the autopsy photos of President Kennedy. If I am correct you have viewed those photos at the national archives?

Yes.

Do you believe, from what you originally saw at Parkland, in regards to the President's wounds, that the autopsy photos have been tampered with, or do you think that they are pulling President Kennedy's scalp up and it's hiding the wound in the back of his head?

That's what I thought (the latter option) because one of the pictures shows that the back part of his head was intact, and I had seen it blown out. But I discounted the significance of that when I first saw that, because when I looked at that picture it looked like the autopsy doctor had pulled a flap of scalp over that hole in his head. I can see his thumb and forefinger in the top of the picture pulling the scalp forward.

But then I was later told by some of the people who were at the autopsy, that no, that had not been a flap pulled up over the wound, but was the way it had been there showing the whole back of head intact.

Well, I knew that wasn't right. I didn't speculate that I may be wrong. No, I knew exactly what that wound looked like and the back of his head was gone on the right side, five or six inches in diameter. I didn't get a complete idea of the wound until many years later when I saw the Zapruder film and I put that together with what I saw in Trauma Room One and it looks to me like he was hit from the front. His head explodes, literally, and he's thrown violently back and to the left.

People always ask me if I saw a wound from the front; no, I did not because I didn't get a chance to examine his body that carefully. All I got to see was that massive hole in the back of his head, so I'm making the assumption that there was probably a smaller hole somewhere near the hairline of the right side of his scalp and it blew out the right side of his skull.

Is it possible for a bullet to hit someone in the right side of their head and blow out the same side?

It's possible, but not probable.

People argue that if President Kennedy was shot from the grassy knoll, the left side of his head would have been blown out, and not the right, because the entry of the bullet would have come from the right hand side where the knoll is located. What do you make of that assessment?

No, people who say that really don't have any conception of bullet wounds.

Do you think you couldn't see the entry wound because of the damage on his head?

It was bloody and there was a lot of hair, and also we didn't get a chance to examine him closely. All we saw him was five minutes, and all I could see was the back of his head.

What do you think happened for the rear wound to be covered up in the autopsy photos?

Well, I think it's only that one picture. I discounted that picture because I thought someone was pulling the scalp over it, but someone told me they weren't, but it sure looked like they were. I think they were, so I was not mystified by saying it doesn't look like what I saw. The wounds that I saw when that flap is not covering them were just the kind of same wounds that I had seen in Trauma Room One. That picture where they are pulling the flap up was the only one out of several photos, which didn't jive with what I saw.

Do you think they didn't want people to see the wound in the back of the head?

No. I think whenever you make a series of autopsy photos, if they were trying to do that they wouldn't have shown any of the open wounds that weren't covered with the flap and it was apparent that he had a big hole in the back of his skull on the right side. I don't think they were trying to cover it up or they wouldn't have shown those other photos.

You have been quoted as saying that you have seen the president's autopsy photos that show a great defect in the back of his head?

Yes. I've seen them, and that's what I saw.

Is it possible that if JFK has been shot from behind and nowhere else, that he could have a wound like you saw in the back of his head?

That can happen, sure. In other words, if he was shot from above and the bullet came down from above at about a 45 degree angle, it's possible that that hole could have been made that way. But putting the whole thing together, after I had seen the Zapruder film as well as what I had seen directly, it seemed clear to me that he was shot from the front, from the grassy knoll, because of the way his body was thrown backward and to the left; that was consistent with my view of the wound when I first saw it, that this was an exit rather than an entrance wound.

Do you think President Kennedy was shot from the front?

I think he was. That's my view of it. Other people don't agree with that, but that's where I think he was shot from. And as you recall from the Zapruder film, a whole crowd of people, right after the last shot was fired, ran toward the grassy knoll and the picket fence because that's where the crowd had heard the bullet being fired from.

Is it medically possible that there was a shot from the front?

I think so, yeah.

Were all of the doctors who saw President Kennedy at Parkland Hospital given a fair chance to testify before the Warren Commission and the House Select Committee on Assassinations?

Some of us were interviewed by the Warren Commission. Dr. Perry was considered a principal witness, and he went to Washington and testified before the Warren Commission group. Those of us who were secondarily involved, like me, were interviewed by representatives. Arlen Specter was the lawyer representing the Warren Commission who interviewed me at Parkland Hospital in the administrator's office a short time after the assassination.

As far as the House Select Committee on Assassinations, were you allowed to testify to them?

Yes, I talked to them.

Do you know why some people claim that the Dallas doctors weren't given a fair shake by the House Select Committee on Assassinations?

There was no attempt to cover up my testimony. I don't think anyone tried to suppress our testimony.

So, was there any inclination of a cover up like the movie "JFK" portrays?

No. That dissension is, of course, about whether he was shot from the front or the back, and that thought may be a very honest difference of opinion by those who study and write about it.

Why is the Kennedy assassination important to my generation?

I think it's important to the whole nation, and will be, just like Lincoln's assassination. We need to keep track of what's going on. So, it's very critical to know about those things and know about who's representing us in the government.

Do you have any other thoughts?

Well, you're talking about a conspiracy to murder the President. I can't say from what I've seen, one way or the other, whether there was or wasn't a conspiracy. I certainly don't have enough information to say whether it was a lone nut or a carefully laid plan. I think you can find things in the entire massive amount that's been written on this that will support the lone gunman or a conspiracy where there was more than one gunman. We may never know that. We know there was a conspiracy in Lincoln's assassination, but we don't know who the head man was behind that assassination.

Dan Hardway

What business does a young person have investigating a presidential assassination? Just ask Dan Hardway. Mr. Hardway was a 24 year old law student at Cornell University when Chief Counsel of the House Select Committee on assassinations, Robert Blakey, hired him as an investigator for Congress's inquiry into President Kennedy's assassination. Mr. Hardway was tasked with looking into Mexico City, and the CIA's response to JFK's assassination.

Although the CIA thought dealing with a young law student would be below their standard, Mr. Hardway showed them differently. He was able to uncover a lot of evidence, and he was also quite successful in prying documents from the government's hands. Together with his co-worker, Edwin Lopez, they wrote the report, *"Oswald, the CIA, and Mexico City."*

If you are a young person who wants to make a change in history, you can be encouraged by Mr. Hardway's story. He was the David vs. Goliath of this case, and he sunk his stones directly into the CIA's disinformation machinery. Let's take a deeper look into his experiences and thoughts about the assassination.

How are you involved within the JFK assassination?

I worked for the House Select Committee on Assassination in 1977-1978. I was on the JFK side. I was assigned to Team Five, which was the investigation of the relationship or any possible relationship between Oswald and the CIA, and the investigation of the intelligence agency's performance responding to the assassination.

What is your overall view on the House Select Committee? Do you feel it was an overall success or that it could have been better?

Obviously it could have been better, but under the circumstances I think they did a fantastic job. I can't say anything about the Dr. King side. I don't know anything about that. But, on the JFK side, again, given the limitations and recognizing that I'm speaking mainly about the investigation into the intelligence agencies with which I'm familiar, I think we did a very good job under the circumstances that existed at the time.

The reason I asked that is because some have raised concerns about the House Select Committee on Assassinations, even going as far as accusing it of being a cover up of the Warren Report. Because you were personally involved in the investigation of the HSCA, would you want to comment on that?

Well, I think a lot of that is people looking back with the hindsight of what's known now, and looking back in hindsight, you know, even Bob Blakey says we were duped. But, you can't really judge a historical event by what's been read into it 30 years after it happened. When you look at it like that you have to try and understand what was going on at the time, and where we were, and what we were able to accomplish. But what we were able to accomplish was slightly remarkable.

As a matter of fact, the fact that there are segregated files, which are now becoming public, is due largely to our efforts, and Bob Blakey's work in requiring as apart of the agreement he had with the CIA to have those records segregated. So, the ARRB (Assassination Records Review Board), to the extent that they had records, a lot of those records were there because of what we did.

If you go back and put yourself in the place that we were at when we started, to illustrate it, the October 8th cable from Mexico City from headquarters reporting Oswald's contact with the consulate was highly expurgated. The only copies available were highly expurgated copies, and that's where we started. We started out trying to fill in blanks on those, just like critics did until we could access the documentation.

The other aspect to that is that you've got to understand the political situation as it existed in 1976-77. The Committee was in political shambles when Bob Blakey took it over. For whatever reason you think caused those, whoever you want to blame, whether it be one of the Congressmen, the Agency subverting it, if you want blame the attorneys who were trying to run the staff at the time, or whatever - it's irrelevant at this point who was to blame in the context of the question you asked - but if you look at that kind of political context, this was an incredibly difficult situation that we found ourselves in. We had to try to survive given that political firestorm that Bob Blakey was inheriting and the limits that it created on him, on us. When you go back and look at it in that context and then go back and look at what we did it, it wasn't anywhere close to perfect, it wasn't anywhere close to ideal. But then again, given what we knew, and the time frame we were in, we did a fantastic job.

In your area of expertise, you focused more on Oswald's possible intelligence connections with the CIA's Mexico City operation, is that correct?

That was my primary area of responsibility, yeah.

As far as that incident, what did you learn about Oswald's possible relationship with the CIA?

There were all kinds of question. At the time, based on Mexico City, we didn't really do a whole lot of analysis of whether or not it showed a relationship with the CIA. And, part of the reason why the Lopez report doesn't really go into that is because at the time we did not really have a positive identification on Maurice Bishop; Antonio Veciana wouldn't give us a positive ID at that time. This is probably my fault. I was not aware that the CIA was planning on exporting the anti-Fair Play for Cuba Committee propaganda operations overseas, and I didn't make that connection.

As best as I can remember, I did not read the portion of the Church report that reported that at the time. Consequently, in looking at Mexico City, there was all kinds of suspicious stuff going on, but none of it really pointed toward a definite relationship between Oswald and the Agency based on what we had at the time. And if you read the Lopez Report, which the CIA said that it was fallibly speculative and irresponsible, it's actually written in a very measured tone where we tried to not draw any conclusions that weren't warranted by the evidence that we were able to develop.

Our conclusions were stated tentatively because we didn't have absolute proof of things and where we didn't have absolute proof of things, we stated what we had, and so we really didn't get into whether or not Mexico City showed that connection. That aspect is something that I think has developed as a result of subsequent revelations, and subsequent work that's gone a lot further than we were able to do in 1977-78 - work that's been done by Peter Dale Scott and John Newman, Jeff Morley and Dave Talbot…people like that.

Now, in the Mexico City report there is a section about Oswald and the CIA, and Mr. Lopez, who you worked with on the report, is quoted as saying that the CIA "hated it." Do you know anything about that?

Yeah, if you read the Lopez Report, it's written to be a part of the final report. If you notice, in the Lopez Report the conclusions are stated in terms of the Committee's conclusions, not in terms of a researcher's report. It was actually a draft of the section of the final report that was going to be made in reference to Mexico City and the agency's performance in Mexico City. There is a reference in there citing to a section on possible relationships between Oswald and the CIA. That was not something that was written as part of the Mexico City report. That was another section of the final report that was being drafted.

As I understood it, the best I can remember, it was being drafted by Mickey Goldsmith, the head of Team Five, which incorporated work from all the various researchers, attorneys and investigators working on Team Five. In fact, I haven't ever had the time or the resources to do the kind of research at the National Archives that I would like to do after the ARRB's work, but I have seen portions of the draft of that section in records on Mary Ferrell's website. There are portions of that draft that I contributed and there are portions that other people contributed. Whether or not it was finalized and submitted to the CIA in a final draft version, I don't know because I left before the final report was written.

As far as your work with the CIA, how did they treat you?

I didn't work *with* them; I worked *at* their office. They didn't like us. We were brash young kids. We were arrogant and full of ourselves and we were on a mission. They didn't like that. They felt we didn't show them the respect they thought they were entitled to.

Some people say the CIA was offended that you and Mr. Lopez, being so young with no experience in dealing with the CIA, were sent to investigate them. Were you aware of that at the time?

I wasn't really aware of that. I knew that there was antagonism, but you have to break this thing into stages because things changed over the process of the investigation. Initially, when we first went out there, and Bob had negotiated the access agreement that we had, the person we were assigned initially to work with was Regis Blahut, who later became famous because he had, evidently, attempted to steal or conceal the Committee autopsy photos, but that was later. Initially he was working with Eddie and me at the CIA and was our contact for file requests and things of that nature.

That was very early on in the process, but after we had an office established at the CIA they had a little internal room somewhere with no windows, that was not very big that they locked me and Eddie in all day, or me if I was ever alone or Eddie if he was ever alone. And, in all honesty, Regis treated us decently with requests about documents, never indicated a dislike for us personally or anything. As a matter of fact, he tried to pitch me on a career with the CIA after the committee was done; he told me he thought I would make a great agent. I don't know if that was an authorized pitch or not.

I went back to the House offices and reported that with an outside contacts report as was appropriate. I don't know whatever happened to that; haven't seen it since.

After Regis got transferred down, we were assigned two other clerks and they were fairly - I hate to sound condescending, but they appeared - nondescript. But that's what they were, they appeared to be clerks. They treated us kindly as far as I can tell. At the time, evidently, they thought we were rude to them. We did pressure them to try and keep the fires going underneath them to try to get documents and keep things moving quickly. And again, looking through some of the Mary Ferrell documents, I have found some documents containing complaints about us being rude.

We really didn't have a problem with the way they were treating us until Joannides and Breckenridge took over. And at that point it wasn't really how they treated us, as it was how they cut us off. And although I had met Scott Breckenridge and had interaction with him quite frequently, I only met Joannides once. Basically, I think the reason I met him is because he came in when he wanted to gloat. They gave me a highly expurgated document, a very highly expurgated document, and he just got enjoyment out of that.

Since we're already on that topic. Lone nut advocates claim the reason why Joannides was called out of retirement was not to hide a conspiracy, but to protect assets and self-interest. What do you make of that assessment?

That's not justification whatsoever for withholding the file.

Some people raise the point that the CIA saw their selves only accountable to the president, and therefore not accountable to the legislative law. What do you think of that?

That's a very interesting legal position. It's also a legal position that is subject to a lot of debate. I mean, the CIA was created by an act of the legislature, they are subject to the legislature, and they are subject to the laws of the land. They take a position out of the National Security Act which they say exempts them from the normal criminal law. That reading by CIA advocates and CIA attorneys is a very, very controversial reading, and a long stretched presumption based on very straightforward language in the act.

I personally don't think that it's justified. I don't think that, in a nation of laws, any institution is above the law. I understand that is their position and that they have acted that way since they were founded, and no one has ever really ever stopped them, or called them on it. That's a part of the problem we have in the country today.

The idea that what they gave us they gave us by grace basically denies the rule of the people. I mean, Congress is the representative of people of the United States. The ultimate force of government is in the people, at least theoretically, and for the CIA to say that they are not responsible to Congress is absurd. That's a totally totalitarian idea. It should be foreign to our experience, foreign to our way of thinking and foreign to our law.

So, for the record, no matter what the CIA's excuse is, if Congress requests files from them during an investigation, they should hand those files over.

Absolutely. I think that the CIA has to be accountable. Every institution of government has to be accountable.

As for the remaining files the CIA is withholding, do you buy the argument that they are hiding these files because they are protecting certain assets?

No. I don't buy that. If that were, in fact, the case then there is no basis or justification of withholding the documents in full.

What's in those files that they don't want us to see?

I don't know. I'd like to see them so I can see why they are holding them back. But, you know, Joannides supposedly came out of retirement to work with us, and at that time he was involved in a counter-espionage operation that culminated in the firing of a co-worker in Indiana in which the co-worker was eventually convicted of espionage in April of 1977. That's before he came to work as our liaison in May. So, he may have been retired. He may have been called out. But, he may not have been "retired" either. Like Bob Blakey said, at this point I don't believe anything the CIA said…nothing.

Conspiracy theorists are often written off as crackpots. What do you think of that?

Why do you call them conspiracy theorists? You know where that term came from? It came from a 1967 memorandum that went to every CIA station around the world telling them how to counter Warren Commission critics. That's where the term got wide spread usage. They are given a bad name like that because of the CIA's disinformation campaign.

Exactly, that's what I'm getting to. From what you have seen, is it not logical to assume the CIA is hiding something relating to the assassination? I mean, it's a known fact that there is at least a conspiracy within the CIA to hide something.

Well, okay, why do we want to go jump to conclusions without evidence? I would much rather maintain an open mind, and see the evidence. I'm not trying to prove a theory. I don't have a theory. But, I've got questions that aren't answered that raise troubling issues, very troubling issues. If there's nothing in those issues, there shouldn't be any reason to not release the documentation.

Let me back up. When we first started working for the HSCA, before we got access to unexpurgated files, we had what had been released at that point through the Freedom of Information Act in highly expurgated form, just like everybody else. If you go back and read a lot of the critical work in the late 60s and early 70s a lot of people were guessing and trying to fill in the blanks of these expurgated documents. They were building theories based upon their guesses and then filling in the blank information they didn't have.

Once we got the unexpurgated access, we were able to fill in those blanks, some of the blanks, and consequently we were able to dismiss a lot of the stuff that had been speculated about up to that point. But, it raised a whole set of additional questions, and led us to a whole set of additional documents with questions that we had that we wanted to investigate.

I don't want to go back to that position we were in the 60s and early 70s, where we're trying to build theories or guesses based on what was withheld. Until we see those documents, there's no reasonable basis to do that, and yeah, if we did stuff like that then there's proper critiques.

If the CIA is withholding files, and those files are somehow connected to the man who allegedly murdered the president, then that's good reason for suspicion, is it not?

It's a good reason to ask questions, but there also may be innocent explanations. Let's take a fact for example. David Phillips' assets ran all kinds of disinformation after the assassination trying to link Oswald to Cuba and Russia, and trying to blame the Cubans and Russians for the assassination. It's a fact that you can trace a lot of those reports back to Phillips' agents.

Well, one possible explanation of that would be that it was a disinformation operation ran by David Phillips. It's a classic David Phillips operation. It fits the MO perfectly, but we don't have any absolute proof of any kind that that is actually the explanation of what happened.

There are also other possible explanations. One of the other possible explanations is that most of these guys were very highly motivated anti-communist's and they may have very well taken advantage of the opportunity on their own and just tried to exploit it. Or, Phillips may have run an operation like that, but it may have been to take advantage of the assassination and it does not necessarily indicate any foreknowledge or involvement. It even might indicate that there was foreknowledge and involvement, and that it was an operation that was laid down and planned in advance.

Right now we don't have enough information that will tell us exactly what happened. In all honesty, if you want to move this thing forward you have to take a very non-speculative approach, and try to be reasonable, in your analysis of what you find.

So, it's important to not read too far into the rabbit trial before we have all the facts?

That's right.

Vincent Bugliosi, in his famous book, "Reclaiming History," makes it seem as if

Oswald was a simple, sociopath character with nearly no associations outside of Marina Oswald, her associates or his co-workers. Is that a credible assessment?

No.

Why not?

On that I would just refer you to John Newman's book, *Oswald and the CIA*. I mean you can start with the way that his files were handled at the Agency. You can go from there to the fact that he was babysat by George de Mohrenschildt, someone that has been acknowledged to have CIA connections. The person who got the Mexico travel visa immediately before Oswald, and was standing in line in front of Oswald, was an acknowledged CIA agent. I mean, there's too many possible connections to just flat out say that there was no one that he had connections with.

Secondly, we don't have all the evidence yet.

Would you disagree with Mr. Posner's title, "Case Closed"?

Oh, absolutely. I think that's kind of a silly question. If the case were closed, it would have been closed. I don't think anyone besides Posner, Bugliosi, and the guy on Fox, O'Reilly, thinks the case is closed.

Switching gears real quickly. Let's talk about David Atlee Phillips. He is someone a lot of people believed was either involved in the assassination, or knew something about it and covered it up after the fact. You interviewed him personally. What did you make of him?

Yep. I also prepared the attorneys who did his second deposition with the committee. I was present for that as well.

Gaeton Fonzi, in his book, described how you were able to expose some of Mr. Phillips' lies. What did you think of this man, your read on him, and his responses to your questions?

He's a hard man to read. A very hard man to read.

So, he didn't give a lot up?

No, he gave a lot up. You just don't know what to make out of what he gave up.

Let me explain that. David Phillips was an actor as well as an agent. He acted in amateur plays evidently most of his life. He seemed very self controlled, fairly sophisticated, eloquent and intelligent. In the course of our interview with him he was surprised that Gaeton was there.

Gaeton wasn't supposed to be there. Gaeton was in town and found out that I was doing the interview, and I was more than happy to have Gaeton sit in on it. It was quite a long interview, and I have not seen a copy of the memos I wrote on that interview anywhere on Mary Ferrell, or any official copy of it. There is a bootleg copy of it circulating somewhere in the critical community, and I managed to get a copy of that. There was a very large briefing book that I prepared for that interview which I have not seen and it's unfortunate because the memo of the interview is not really totally comprehensible unless you have the briefings I've referred to.

I say this because the memo of the interview is basically a summary of certain parts within it. One of the things that I wanted to get to was the disinformation campaign that was ran after the assassination, or at least what appears to be a disinformation campaign. When Mr. Phillips had testified before the committee, the second time in executive session under oath, we took him through a lot of his former agents and things of that nature and questioned him about his relationships and continuing relationships with those people. Some of them he denied, and some of them he admitted to.

After this, I went back and I had identified these people by the time I had interviewed him in August for the last time, and I knew it was going to be the last shot I had at him. I identified the people that were sources of stories right after the assassination, in the first few weeks or first months. I don't remember my time frame, but it was not long after the assassination. I pulled those stories. I requested CIA files on them. I was able to tie almost every single one of them into being either activated by David Phillips, or involved in an operation of David Phillips.

I started going down the list and confronting him with this information, and what we knew about it, and the further I got down the list the more nervous he appeared to become. At one point, he had three or four cigarettes lit at one time, and I got to the end of my list and basically, I didn't have an ace in the hole. Now, if you want to speculate a little bit and spend some time thinking about what would have happened if I would have thrown out Joannides and the DRE (Directorio Revolucionario Estudiantil or Student Revolutionary Directorate) at that point, but I didn't because we didn't have that information at the time.

So, we switched at that point to the connections that we had that connected him to Veciana. The first one we asked about was the Bishop alias, and at that point when we asked about it he blew up. At the time and since then, I've looked back on it, and I've asked myself several times, *was he really nervous, or was he making a show of things?*

And when he blew up on that question, and started raving about not wanting to be accused of being Bishop, and thinking that that issue was dead and behind us and everything, again I had to ask, *was he really upset or was he putting on a show for us.*

I've got my own personal opinion on those things, but I've gotten nothing to base them on. They're purely speculative.

Right. However, if anyone deserves to have a speculation, it's you since you were right in front of the man, and you interrogated him personally.

My opinion has changed over the years.

How so?

Well, on whether or not he was actually nervous. Initially I thought it may have been an act, but with what I've come to discover since then, especially about Joannides, I think the man was scared to death.

I've always wondered what he was scared of. Why was he so nervous? He is not the kind of person that would have been made nervous by a possible perjury indictment. I don't think he was scared of me. I don't think he was scared of the Committee. I mean, he lied frequently and often to the Committee.

You have to wonder what would scare a man like that.

Maybe he was worried you were about pull something out that would expose him?

Even if I were, why would that worry him?

Well, he did always seem worried that he would be implicated in the assassination.

Well, he already was. Why would being able to tie him to all these different disinformation operations scare him? Is it possibly because of a lot of people had to be thinking we were going to find out about Joannides and the DRE? With that being the case, what was he scared of? Why did he get so nervous?

Why do you think he was so nervous?

It's impossible to know, but he was scared of something that was threatening enough to cause him fear.

In some of the conferences you have spoke at I have heard you speculate that maybe

Mr. Phillips was a case officer type, or connected to Lee Oswald in some way. Then the president is killed by Oswald and Phillips is put into the position of where he sees that the man he was involved with impulsively killed the president.

Allegedly.

Right. Allegedly. Do you still think that's possible?

That's a possibility. Like I said before, when you look at the facts we have, there are various possible explanations.

Mr. Phillips lied repeatedly of his knowledge about Oswald in Mexico?

It isn't that he lied about not knowing anything about it. Rather, He lied about what *was* known about it. He lied about the Mexico cables and the Mexico operations in his first testimony. We caught him up in those lies in his second testimony.

Could you briefly explain what a cable is?

A cable is information sent from Mexico City to headquarters reporting information. Specifically it was the October 8th cable reporting Oswald initial contact. David Phillips initially testified that he signed off on that. He had been very much involved in getting the information out and getting it done at the station. He said he had to argue with certain people at the agency to get them to do their job and etc., etc., etc. And he wasn't even there. He wasn't in Mexico City when the cables went out.

Do you believe Lee Harvey Oswald ever was in Mexico City?

I have no idea. From all indications it does appear that he was. You know, I think there's a good chance that he was impersonated or that documentation was falsified. At this point it's very hard for us to tell.

There are good indications that someone may have been imitating him, but then again we're dealing with the CIA and I don't believe anything they tell me, and I really don't believe all their documentation anymore. Someone speaking broken Russian claimed to be Oswald. Someone who apparently was supposed to have been Oswald spoke Spanish. The Russian was bad, the Spanish was good. Oswald didn't speak Spanish, but he did speak decent Russian. The tape containing one of the intercepted conversations existed at least up until 1972 or so. The people who heard the tapes said it didn't sound like Oswald.

There were photographs that were obtained that have never been produced. I'm convinced of that. There were photographs obtained by the impulse camera at the Cuban consulate. I'm sure that some would say I'm speculating, and to a certain point I am. But, if you're applying a legal standard of proof, I think I could prove that that photograph existed with circumstantial evidence. In a criminal case it may not be proved down to a reasonable doubt, but in a civil case it's certainly provable with the preponderance of the evidence.

And there may be various reasons why that photograph was never produced. One of those reasons is the possibility that it wasn't Oswald, it was an imposter. Another reason may be that he was with someone else. We don't know. But the evidence indicates that even if Oswald was there that someone else was pretending to be Oswald, or impersonating him.

Then you can take it to the next level and question what you're seeing, which is something you always have to do when you go down the intelligence rabbit hole. You know, we've got CIA officers who testified as to hearing the tapes, and then scrapping them, so we don't know for sure that the fakery, if there was fakery, is or isn't true. We don't know. But, we do know someone claiming to be Oswald visits the consulate, and there's reasonable evidence that this was indeed Oswald. There's also reasonable evidence he was impersonated. Either or both may be true.

Do you believe the cable about Oswald in Mexico was created after the assassination?

I don't know. I don't think so. It may have been, but I don't know. A lot of people remembered another cable that's never been produced.

Oswald allegedly met with some students down in Mexico that were pro-Castro, and I believe I read you wanted to track these people down during your investigation, and the CIA frustrated your efforts?

Yep.

In light of that, do you believe it's possible that Oswald was with someone else in Mexico, and the CIA's cameras showed that?

I think it's possible, yes. Tony Summers actually found a guy who said that Oswald also hooked up with a Quaker group down in Mexico City. The person he interviewed said that he linked up with one other guy who had a motorcycle that gave him a ride back to the Cuban consulate that day.

I know Oswald was introverted, but I have always found it hard to believe that

Oswald went to Mexico and did nothing but stare at the wall.

Oh yeah, he did other things, obviously.

Gaeton Fonzi believed that David Atlee Phillips was Maurice Bishop.

Oh, I think we have strong proof that he was.

So, you believe David Atlee Phillips was Maurice Bishop?

Absolutely.

Do you believe that Antonio Veciana is a credible witness?

Absolutely. He has been credible consistently, with only one exception and that was his refusal to identify David Atlee Phillips as Bishop, up until last year.

So, he has identified David Atlee Phillips as Maurice Bishop?

Yes. He has stated unequivocally that David Atlee Phillips was Maurice Bishop.

So, that would lead us to believe that Antonio Veciana did see Lee Harvey Oswald with David Atlee Phillips in Dallas?

Yep. In late August or early September (1963).

That would be explosive to say the least.

I think so, but no one paid any attention to it.

Robert Blakey takes a lot of heat over how he handled the assassination investigation. I wanted to ask you if you think Mr. Blakey was fair in his investigation.

Yes.

You've been accused of being cynical.

(Laughs) I'd like to know who accused me of that.

Well, it was brought up on one of your C-SPAN conference videos on the assassination.

Oh, yeah, that was at the end of that panel discussion up in Pittsburg, probably.

Do you think it's smart, in light of how the government has reacted to the case, to be cynical at this point?

I think the American people are very cynical about the Agency and the assassination.

Would you say it's wise to always be skeptical from here on out?

Well, I think the safest move at this point is to not believe anything the CIA tells you.

Do you believe there was a conspiracy to murder President Kennedy?

I believe, based on the available evidence that I have seen, that there was a conspiracy to kill John F. Kennedy.

I believe it's your opinion that a government institution, like a congressional committee can't investigate itself. Do you still believe that?

In that speech I gave, actually that was a part of a panel discussion I believe, and in that panel discussion what I said is that living as a culture of secrecy and allowing that secrecy is a cancer that's destroying our freedoms. And it destroys any kind of accountability and it destroys any kind of stability of a congressional investigation, or even a criminal prosecution to get to the bottom of that type.

David Talbot calls for a civilian panel to take the case over. My question for you is that if a government institution, like a congressional committee, can't adequately investigate something like the murder of a president, then how can a civilian panel do it without subpoena power? What can a citizen do?

Well, I think what the citizens of the United States have to do is that they have to demand an end of the secrecy and demand the accountability of the CIA and the other intelligence agencies. That doesn't mean that everything they do has to be immediately disclosed, but it does mean that in everything that they do, they can be held accountable.

A system has to be in place which will end this type of perpetual and internal secrecy that allows them not only to hide state secrets, but allows them to hide their own misdeeds and malfeasance. There is no place for something like that in a free and open democratic society. It is totally incompatible with what we are as a country.

If it is some action that they think that within five years they can't stand up and publicly say they committed, they shouldn't be doing it anyways. Because the only thing were doing by allowing this kind of secrecy to continue is allowing them to be totally unaccountable, not only in the interest of national security, but also in their own personal interest as well. You can't give people that kind of power in a free and open society.

Is that why you believe that finding out all the facts about the Kennedy assassination is still important in 2015?

Absolutely.

Do you believe we will ever get all of the files on the assassination, and if you do what advice do you have for future researchers?

Two questions there. Do I think that we will ever get all the files? I think that not all the files still exist. Do I think that we'll ever get all the files that still exist? Maybe.

What advice would I give future researchers? We're moving from any possibility of investigation. The last remaining living witnesses are rapidly dying. You know the person who holds the documents, holds the history, and at this point the only thing I can tell a researcher from basically a historical viewpoint is to be very, very, very careful in the handling of the details in the remaining documents.

The devil's always in the details. Make very good notes. Become comprehensive in the coverage of an area, and analyze everything with very skeptical eye. Do the analysis with the view of sifting through the contradictions you're going to find within the documents.

You know, that was one of the techniques that I think Eddie and I, I'm sure it's been done in other investigations, but we were kind of reinventing the wheel because we were so young and inexperienced. One of the things that I did was look at routing slips, and filing instructions. A lot of the stuff I got that led me to believe there was a photograph came out of different files.

You know, be very careful in your analysis. Work hard. Be fair. Structure it. Keep an open mind. Don't immerse yourself totally in just this one area. Familiarize yourself with operations and how they go down. Familiarize yourself with the people. You're going to see the people recurring throughout history exercising some familiar patterns. That's something Peter Dale Scott does well. John Newman also does it well, and so does Larry Hancock. You know, you're going to see Henry Hecksher. You're going to see David Phillips. You're going to see Ted Shackley. You're going to all these guys popping up in different places, doing very similar things.

Do you believe if you and Mr. Lopez wouldn't have worn flip flops and would have combed your hair we might have solved the assassination?

No. You only got a little bit of how we offended them with appearance. I wasn't aware at the time of the Tom Brown axiom that, *why offend with appearance when you can offend with substance*, so we were trying to do both. But I didn't wear flip flops.

What happened to President Kennedy on Nov. 22, 1963?

I think that any reasonable jury on that would still be out. We're still waiting for the prosecution and defense to rest their cases.

So, do you think it's safe to sit on the fence until we have all of the evidence?

Well, no. I think you can form a conclusion upon the available evidence, if you want to do that. I think that based on the available evidence it's pretty much uncontroversial that there was a conspiracy. Uh, I mean, you know the only credible evidence on the acoustics is that there were two shooters, at least two shooters. I think that to anyone that's reasonable in his or her scientific approach to that it's a settled issue.

I mean, you know, the lone nutters are still trying to discredit that, but they're not having much success with any kind of credible scientific presentation. They can play games with the analysis and with the science and try to cause it to be questioned, but looking at it as a trial lawyer, in the preponderance of the evidence, we win that argument.

There was a conspiracy. The circumstantial evidence is there. Who the members of that conspiracy were, it's an open question. It's the same thing. It's incontrovertible that there was a conspiracy to cover up key facts, and to blame Oswald. That doesn't necessarily mean that there was a conspiracy to kill the president, but there was definitely a conspiracy to conduct a cover up.

That conspiracy included Lyndon Johnson. That conspiracy included J. Edgar Hoover. That conspiracy included James Angleton and Allen Dulles. The technical legal term for that is obstruction of justice. That happened. From there you can form what opinion you like based on the evidence.

Walter Cronkite, in one of the statements he made, I don't remember if it was after Oswald was killed, or whether it was on one of the stations commenting on the Kennedy assassination later on, said that the American people are the jury in this case, and you know, today the jury thinks that they haven't been told the truth, I'd say.

Marie Fonzi

Mr. Hardway spoke a lot about Antonio Veciana, the former Cuban exile who told House Select Committee staffer Gaeton Fonzi that he saw Lee Harvey Oswald with his former CIA case officer in Dallas shortly before the President was murdered. This case officer was alleged to have been former CIA agent David Atlee Phillip, who at the time was using the alias "Maurice Bishop." It was "Bishop" who Veciana said was with Oswald in Dallas.

Mrs. Marie Fonzi, Gaeton Fonzi's wife, was gracious enough to provide the author with a copy of Veciana's confession to her that David Atlee Phillips was indeed the mysterious "Maurcie Bishop" after all.

Mrs. Fonzi credits Joaquin Goday for putting her in contact with Veciana.

November 22. 2013

Dear Marie Fonzi:

You may publish the following statement from me:

"Maurice Bishop, my CIA contact agent was David Atlee Phillips. Phillips or
Bishop was the man I saw with Lee Harvey Oswald in Dallas on September 1963."

Best Regards,

Antonio Veciana

The Lone Assassin Theory

In this section we will hear from those who believe Lee Harvey Oswald was the lone assassin in Dealey Plaza on November 22, 1963. In 1964, the Warren Commission came to the conclusion that President Kennedy had been killed by Lee Harvey Oswald alone, and that Jack Ruby, the nightclub owner who had murdered Oswald after he was taken into police custody, had also acted alone. Simply put, the Warren Commission found there was no evidence for a conspiracy, and as far as the government was concerned the case was closed.

The experts of the Lone Assassin Theory agree that Oswald was the man who fired the fatal shots in Dealey Plaza. Of course, these researchers believe they can prove their case through hard evidence. They raise concerns about Lee Harvey Oswald's character, and they ask us to explain who he really was outside of all the hype that surrounds him. They point us to the alleged evidence that is piled sky high against Oswald, and they try to use logic to confirm the Warren Commission's conclusions that Jack Ruby was not tied to any conspirators either. They also believe they can prove that all of the shots that struck the president came from Lee Harvey Oswald's rifle, and they find no evidence for a second shooter on the grassy knoll.

Did Lee Harvey Oswald, out of a hatred for America and a need to be validated on the world stage, murder President Kennedy in broad daylight? If that is the case, why has there been so much controversy surrounding such a simplistic conclusion? Is there any rational way to explain the controversy surrounding the medical evidence of the president's wounds? What about Jack Ruby? What drove him to murder Oswald on national television? Why is this case important to continuing generation if Oswald acted alone? These experts believe they have the answers to these questions and more. Let's see if that is the case.

Dale K. Myers

Dale K. Myers is an Emmy Award winning computer animator, and a very intelligent JFK assassination researcher. His book, *With Malice: Lee Harvey Oswald and the Murder of Officer J. D. Tippit*, dives extensively into the circumstances surrounding Lee Oswald's alleged murder of Dallas police Officer J.D. Tippit.

When I first met Dale Myers I felt as if he was a little skeptical of my motive in interviewing him. This skepticism, however, was not unfounded after I heard about the backlash he has received because he believes Lee Harvey Oswald killed President Kennedy alone. Sadly, people miss out on a treasure trove of information because they refuse to speak him.

I'll be honest, I was surprised at what Mr. Myers really believed about this case versus what I had been told he believed by second hand sources. He provided this book with a lot of insight in regards to Officer Tippit's murder, and he also laid out a systematic case for Lee Oswald's guilt in firing the rifle in Dealey Plaza. No matter what you believe, I hope you approach this interview with an open mind. My generation need not join in on the back biting of the past. You can learn from those you disagree with, and do it respectfully. Mr. Myers calls for us to take a hard look at first hand sources before we believe in any certain theory about this case. I think that is a fair approach.

What is your expertise in the JFK assassination?

I would say my work on the Tippit shooting, and the computer work that I did on the Kennedy murder, the computer work being my professional background. I basically took my profession and married it with my interest in this case. But, when I first got into this case, which was back in 1975, I was particularly drawn to the Tippit shooting, so I spent most of my time looking at that aspect of the case, and sort of ventured into the Dealey Plaza stuff only because of my profession. I thought that I could bring something to the party that hadn't been done before.

Could you briefly describe what you brought to the case through your profession?

Well, when I got interested in the case in 1975, I was in broadcast radio. Around the mid 1980s I got into video production, and then in the early 1990s I got into computer animation, which I've been doing freelance ever since. At that time computer tools for the masses were pretty rudimentary, and there were no schools, for instance, but back when I first started in 1990, and during those three years between '90 and '93, I could see the potential for a computer animation and an application that would actually solve the questions I had of the shooting in Dealey Plaza.

I first got interested in this case when I saw a bootleg copy of the Zapruder film, which had been floating around since about 1969. Penn Jones, you're probably familiar with him, was selling them down in Texas in a bootleg 8 millimeter film format. So, I got a hold of a copy of that, and after seeing it, I decided to investigate the facts of the case.

At that time the film had not been broadcast on national television. Anyone who has seen the film knows that in its original form the film is hand held and shaky. It's very difficult, when Kennedy and Connally come out from behind the sign, to see exactly what's happening. So, it occurred to me, after seeing the film, if there was only a way that you could smooth out that action, that you could remove the hand held nature of Zapurder's camera from the film, then you could see more clearly exactly what the film had captured, and at that time there was really no way to do that.

I actually toyed around with the idea of getting a couple of friends and some folding chairs, and posing them frame by frame to match the film, and then re-photographing them in sort of an animated way so that you could see the actions in a more clear version. In essence, that's really what was the impetus of the idea to do something through computer animation.

In 1993, after having three years of experience with the computer program I was using, it occurred to me that I had a tool that actually could do what I had envisioned almost 20 years earlier, which was to bring the film into the program and basically use it as a projection device, and build a three-dimensional model and match it up to the film. Once you had a match of this hand held, shaky film, frame-by-frame, you could basically look through a brand new camera, and view the assassination without that hand held shakiness, and that in essence is the idea.

And of course, it occurred to me that if you build these models, you build the plaza and the Book Depository and the car, where it's at, its position at any given moment as seen in the Zapruder film. Then you could also do measurements, as to how far they are from the building at the time of this reaction or that reaction, and the difference in position between them, and how are they rotated and so on. You could actually do a trajectory analysis. You could line up the wounds and project them; much like the House Select Committee did in 1978.

They did it on paper with mathematical equations. What I was doing was basically sort of the same thing, but I was doing it from a visual standpoint. The advantage that I had, that they did not have, was that the best they could do was do a pretty good guesstimate as to the position of Kennedy and Connally based on stereoscopic viewpoints and the different things that they were using mathematically. But, what I could do, is that I could actually use the Zapruder film, actually project it onto the models, and I could position them in the car exactly as they were within the tolerances that you have.

I mean, it's an 8 mm film frame, something considerably smaller than a postage stamp, which means we are not looking at an IMAX film frame here. We are looking at something that's blurry and so forth. But, there's a reasonable degree of accuracy that you can get from that.

To give you an idea Jacob, if you look at any of the reenactments in live action films, for instance the one Oliver Stone did in *JFK*, and of course the actors are kind of going through the motions that are similar to what we see on the film, but they could never be exact because you could never time out those actions to be exactly like the Zapruder film in a live reenactment.

However, you could with a computer reconstruction, by positioning computer models exactly as they're seen in the film. Well, now you're operating in the 1/18 of second range where you literally have 18 frames a second, 486 frames throughout the whole film. If you match those up, and then play those back in real time, suddenly you're now seeing exactly what would have occurred.

It wouldn't be a recreation as some people call these films, it would be a reconstruction. It would be the same approach that police departments and court rooms have used for scientific evidence in the court room that could be used to prove or disprove something that happened or didn't happen in a certain case.

A lot of people think that when I did this, especially the critics of what I have done, I did an illustration of a theory that I already had. That's not true at all. It's literally a reconstruction of what actually occurred in the plaza as recorded by Zapruder's camera. And once you line up the models and turn that thing on and let it run, the chips fall where they may. Whatever happens, happens. So, the computer simply allowed me to re-photograph what Zapruder captured on film from any angle – in three dimensions.

So, that's the thing that I "brought to the party," if you will. That's something I put on the table that had never been done before, and interestingly enough, despite all of the criticism, no one's ever used the same technique to prove what I did was flawed or that the conclusions I came to are incorrect based on the data captured by Zapruder's camera. In fact, to the contrary, Z-Axis Corporation – one of the leading forensic reconstruction firms in the world vetted my computer work on the Kennedy case and said that I went way beyond what was necessary to prove my findings.

So, you'll hear a lot of kicking and screaming from the diehard conspiracy folks, but not one of them has proven me wrong in the last 20-plus years. And the reason is simple – I'm not wrong.

I do get occasional applause. One of the best responses I ever got was from a physicist that worked at NASA, who emailed me and told me my work was "mind numbingly spectacular" and I had to laugh because it was more mind numbingly challenging than even he suspected. But, you know, he got it.

And of course, on the other end of the spectrum, you have people who absolutely do not know what they're talking about. They are the ones usually on the internet soap box with the biggest megaphones and they're the ones that you have to know to ignore. I'll give you an example Jacob. You're like the third person who has ever even called me in 20 years to talk to me personally and ask me about what I have done. People online look at all those websites and all those YouTube videos that are critiquing what I did, and convincing people that I lied, and I'm an idiot, and don't know what I'm talking about, and I backward engineered it, and all of the other stuff that people say; and not one single person among those folks has ever bothered to pick up the phone and actually talk to the person who did it.

I'm in the phonebook. I'm online. I'm easy to find, as you no doubt found out yourself.

I actually heard you work for the CIA. Is that true?

(Laughs) Yeah, I cash all those checks on a regular basis. You know, it's interesting that I've had that comment thrown at me, and it's also interesting that all the people that disagree with the conspiracy folks refer to people like me as "Lone Nutters." These are all derogatory terms, but you know, you come to accept it. That word gets thrown around a lot. You know, the term "Lone Nutter."

I've sort of gotten use to it and said, "Okay, I know what that means, you're a person who thinks Oswald acted alone." However, most people don't have any idea what I really think about all of that. They just pull from what I did. They say, "Oh, he's just one of those Lone Nutters. He doesn't agree with me, so he is a Lone Nutter." That's not true either, but I'll save that for another question.

I like how you said, in your work, you let the chips fall where they may. Can you further explain that?

That really was it. I don't remember the date, but I remember it was a Wednesday night, it was about 11:30 p.m., and I was about to go to bed. I suddenly realized that I didn't have the model completely done but I had enough in the computer that I could do a trajectory analysis and see where the bullet, that hit Kennedy in the back and then struck Governor Connally, came from.

And of course, I knew I couldn't go to bed then. I had to work that out and see what the answer was. To be honest with you, I was floored when it went back to the sixth floor window of the Book Depository. I really was floored because I wasn't expecting that.

You know how it is. Everybody that reads about this case – including me – starts out as a conspiracy theorist. I don't think anybody can read about this, even back in 1975 when I started, and not be one at some point. I mean 90 percent of the books and magazines, most of the printed material out there, is all conspiracy-oriented. So, if you come into the case cold and all you know is that Kennedy was assassinated and they claim Oswald did it, it takes you about four or five years just to read everything that's out there.

And so, in reading those things, you have no reference point. How do you know what's true or not? All you can do is absorb it. So, at some point a lot of people read all that secondary material and sort of stop investigating and then pontificated upon it for the next 20 years. To me, that is like quitting before you really get started.

In 1980, much like you, I did my own project on the assassination at a radio station. I got the program aired and it won an Associated Press award. What I did was, I basically called up some of the Dallas cops, and took some of the actualities of the time period, audio that aired that weekend, and supplemented it by calling guys like Jim Leavelle and some of the Tippit eyewitnesses and cut it all together. But, what was interesting is that when I actually got out, and stopped reading the background information, and went to the primary sources directly, I found out that most of that background stuff isn't even true. I read quotes from books that weren't even real quotes. I started finding out that I should double check this stuff.

The other thing that swung my head around was that this was not just an obvious conspiracy to everyone at the time, as some people believe, but it was a historical event that happened very quickly, and would take many years to sort out – but that at its heart, what was reported that weekend is exactly what happened.

And more important, that most of the people that write about this are flat out lying. I'll give you an example. One of the books that had the most written about the Tippit shooting at that time, in 1975, was Mark Lane's *Rush to Judgment*. He had a whole chapter dedicated to it, about 14 pages. And of course Mark Lane's position is that it's all a big frame-up. Oswald wasn't even there. The real killer was supposedly a stocky guy with bushy hair. But, in the back of his book were all these footnotes, and of course when you see a book with a lot of footnotes you assume its scholarly, and say to yourself, *He has all the sources he's checked out.*

Well, I went to the sources and he had all these Warren Commission documents. So, I ordered them all from the National Archives, and I started going through them and realized that Lane had taken things out of context and changed the whole meaning of what the original documents said. He didn't show the whole truth of the document to his readers, and flat out lied about what some of them were saying.

So, from that moment forward, I never accepted anything from any book that had been written about the Kennedy assassination, and if the author didn't list footnotes, I wouldn't even spend my money on it. If the book had footnotes, great, but I'm going to check them. The vast majority of the sources cited in conspiracy books don't even support what the authors are claiming. And after putting in as many years as I have researching this case, you can spot the unsubstantiated nonsense instantly.

So, there are a lot of researchers-turned-authors who don't even do investigative work, who just go to the National Archives, and never get out and actually talk to people. You have to get out and talk to people and find out the little details to really put this puzzle together. Unfortunately, many of the people with first hand accounts have passed on in the last few years. So I'm rather pleased that I and several others took the time 30 years ago to gather some of these undocumented accounts.

To me, and you being a younger person who is concerned with real history, it's important to understand that history is just like life, it turns on very small things. It turns on people's emotions and their character idiosyncrasies.

What holes do you see in the theory that Oswald didn't do the shooting in the plaza that day?

To me, common sense tells you that Oswald was shooting alone in the plaza, because if he were a conspirator and had confederates, he would have been whisked away or killed at the scene. In terms of the shooting itself, people talk about how hard of a shot it was, but you could put a monkey up in that window, give him Oswald's rifle and enough ammunition, and he's going to eventually kill somebody.

In fact, I've got a Mannlicher-Carcano, an exact replicate of the one Oswald used, including the scope, and I have ammunition for it. People that say you can't hit anything with it, and that the shooting task was impossible, I just tell them that I've shot that thing personally. It's loud and will blow a pumpkin apart and I'll tell you what, let's go out to a field somewhere and I'll give you a running start, I'll let you get about 90 feet away and I'll fire a few rounds in your direction, and let's just see how lousy of a rifle it really is.

Of course, nobody has ever taken me up on that offer. You've got to ask yourself, why? The answer is simple. Because, I just lay bare the lie that nobody can kill someone with that rifle. That's nonsense.

Oswald could easily have killed someone with that rifle and he did. With three shots, and two hits he killed the president. But, look at what he did afterward. First off, he's not outside the Texas School Book Depository when the president passes by. There's no alibi for him at the time of the shooting. Here's the most politically astute guy, out of everyone in that building, and he's not watching the president roll by his work place? He was no dummy. He'd been to Russia during the height of the Cold War. He was in the U.S. Marine Corps. He went to Mexico and tried to get a visa to Cuba because you couldn't get one in the United States. He was an avid reader of politics, and yet, here's his alleged hero, John F. Kennedy driving by, and by his own account — which he later changed by the way, he remains inside the building.

Can you please explain your thoughts on the Tippit shooting?

What made Tippit call Oswald over? In my book, I was the first one that came out with an idea to answer this question, because something that came up in the eyewitness accounts was compelling. I noticed there was a break in the direction that Oswald was walking. One group of witnesses said that before the shooting Oswald was walking west on the sidewalk, but then another group that had seen Oswald walking just as Tippit's car was pulling alongside him all said he was walking east. So, it occurred to me, *wait a minute, he can't be walking in both directions…..or can he?*

That was really the break for me. So here's Oswald, and I believe this is what happened. He was walking west on the sidewalk, Tippit's coming towards him, driving east. Oswald spots the patrol car. It's been 45 minutes since the Kennedy murder. Now, put yourself in Oswald's shoes. He does not know whether he's been identified or not. He doesn't know whether his fellow employees have turned him in or not. Actually, they're in the process of doing that, saying he's not in the building, but he doesn't know that. He doesn't know if somebody saw him in the window. He doesn't know if they have found his rifle yet. He doesn't know if there is an APB (all points bulletin) on him.

So, he sees the patrol car coming at him on this side street. He spins around quickly and starts walking in the opposite direction. I believe that Tippit spotted this, and thought it was suspicious, and pulled alongside him. Now, Tippit wasn't thinking, "There is the president's assassin," because had he thought that he wouldn't have got caught being gunned down like he did. But, Oswald was suspicious enough to be looked at. Oswald then comes over to the passenger window. There's a brief conversation. By all accounts this conversation lasted 10 to 15 second's – tops. Tippit probably asks Oswald simple questions like *what's going on?*, *where are you headed?*, *you look confused*, etc. Oswald probably says something, and Tippit gets out of the car.

Of course, he's shot before he can get around the side of the car to question Oswald further. I think that he got out of the car because when Oswald leaned down and looked through the window he was sweating. I think he was sweating because he just double timed it, and went 9/10 of a mile in about 12 to 13 minutes. You would have to be running part of the way to accomplish this. He still had his jacket zipped up, and its 68 degrees outside that day. That means Oswald's hair is probably wet, he's probably perspiring. And this is the kind of thing police officers are trained to spot, the unusual.

You or I wouldn't think twice of that, but Tippit, seeing that Oswald was sweating, probably wondered why he wouldn't just take his jacket off? I mean, who is wearing a jacket in that kind of weather? Just take it off while you walk. I think it was probably something as simple as that. But, when Tippit got out of the car, he was distracted. We know that Domingo Benavides, an eyewitness to the shooting, was approaching the scene in his truck. I think Tippit was distracted by the approaching traffic and it was in those few seconds that Oswald pulled the gun and shot him in cold blood.

Why is Oswald shooting a police officer if he's an innocent victim? And, as a side note, there's no evidence of two shooters, or switched shells at the scene. Those are weak arguments made in Oswald's defense built on circular logic. That kind of baseless speculation is basically the same stuff that was written in the first couple of conspiracy books by guys like Mark Lane, and now people are simply regurgitating this stuff over and over again.

So you believe it's undeniable that Oswald shot Officer Tippit?

Absolutely. There is zero evidence that anyone else committed the crime. You have to go back and look at the history of Dallas cop shootings. The last uniformed cop to be shot prior to Tippit, a young police officer named Johnny Sides, was killed 12 years earlier, and the next one, Robert Shipp, was murdered seven years after Tippit. So, a cop shooting in Dallas was highly unusual in 1963, and so when an officer was shot 45 minutes after the assassination of the President, and only two and a half miles from Dealey Plaza, which you can walk in 45 minutes, all the cops and reporters knew the two shootings were tied together. They had to be.

Mrs. Earlene Roberts said that a police car came by her boarding home when Oswald was inside it, not long after the shooting in Dealey Plaza. She claimed this police car beeped its horn twice, like to signal something, and then pulled away, and then Oswald left the boarding house shortly after. What do you make of this testimony?

I've researched this aspect, I believe, more than anyone else. If you go on YouTube, there's a video of her in 1964 that I think local reporter Eddy Barker did, and all you have to do is take one look at this woman and we all know the personality type. Mrs. A.C. Johnson, who was her boss, flat out told the Warren Commission that Earlene Roberts was a talker, that a lot of what Earlene Roberts said was nonsense. And she warned the Warren Commission that basically they shouldn't believe her.

Earlene Roberts also had glaucoma. By her own admission her eyesight wasn't very good. The whole thing about the police car pulling up, she didn't even tell investigators about this until around nine days later. News reporter Hugh Aynesworth speculated that Roberts probably succumbed to all the hype because after all, if you're a relative nobody and suddenly news reporters you've been watching on TV are suddenly at your door interested in what you have to say, you need to say something interesting to keep it going.

As it turns out, her explanation for that car was that it was two officers she knew, and I looked into that. One of the officers she said she knew had resigned from the force in 1957, and the other said he didn't know her. Her explanation didn't even make sense. I've spent the better part of 30 years researching this case and there is nothing about Earlene Roberts' claim that checks out.

And from your computer analysis you believe it's one shooter in the plaza?

It's one shooter. The bottom line is that the shots that hit the car are consistent with the sixth floor depository window as the source of the shots. If you examine the single bullet trajectory, the wounds received by Kennedy and Connally occur at the same time and line up with the sixth floor sniper's nest. So, we already know that one of the shots that hit their target was fired from that location.

Now you go to the head shot. Well, the evidence is not really there to do a trajectory analysis. You have a large exit defect so the bullet could have exited anywhere from within that four-by-six inch area. But, you do have an entrance wound on the back of Kennedy's skull. So, if we take the known shooting location of the first shot that hit Kennedy and Connally, and project a line down from that location to the head wound, and then project that line forward, you find that a straight line trajectory path would exit within the large defect area. So, while you can't do a true trajectory on the head shot, we do know that the physical evidence is consistent with the shot coming from the sixth floor sniper's nest.

It could not have come from the grassy knoll. There's no possible way for that to have occurred and leave no physical evidence. A bullet fired from the grassy knoll area would have exited the left side of Kennedy's skull. There would have been damage there and there isn't. And we know that the entrance wound on the back of the skull came from a rear shot, so it's got to come from somewhere behind the President. And since we know that the shot that passed through Kennedy and Connally — the single bullet — was fired from the sniper's nest, you have to ask yourself, could the second bullet that struck — the fatal headshot — also have come from that location?

As far as the time available is concerned, there's enough time to fire the two shots that hit the president from a single location. From a ballistic standpoint, there were three shells found underneath the sixth floor window, so there's evidence three shots were fired from there — two hits, one miss — and bullet fragments recovered from the car were proven to have been fired from Oswald's Mannlicher-Carcano rifle to the exclusion of all other rifles on the planet.

Finally, are the trajectories of the two shots that struck the president and governor consistent with having been fired from that same location? And again, the answer is, *Yes*.

So, it's a done deal. The evidence is overwhelming and undeniable. One shooter — Lee Harvey Oswald — murdered President Kennedy.

What do you think happened on November 22, 1963 in Dallas? Do you think there was any way there was a conspiracy to murder President Kennedy that day?

Okay, so here is where I stand on the case, and you're asking me the one question that no one bothers to ask. People say, "Yeah, he's a Lone Nutter, and that's all."

No, that's not where I stand. Here's where I stand.

There's only one shooter in the plaza. The entire shooting can be explained by one shooter. There's absolutely no question in my mind that it's Oswald, and he's the sole assassin of both President Kennedy and Officer J.D. Tippit.

So, now the question becomes, which is a completely separate question: Was there a conspiracy? Did somebody put Oswald up to it? Was he working for others, and so forth?

Here's the answer to that question, as I see it.

Oswald had very few friends. He was an outsider, even back in elementary school. You know, he was only 24 years old. The multiple investigations of his life have documented practically everyday, and throughout it a pattern emerges. One of the reasons why I thought the Peter Jennings show, *Beyond Conspiracy,* was good – which I was a part of – was because it spent most of its time talking about Oswald as a person.

See, the conspiracy theorists need to keep Oswald a two-dimensional character. As long as he's a two-dimensional character then they can push him around and make him whatever they want him to be. He can be an FBI informant. He can be a CIA agent. He can be a Secret Service guy. He can be a KGB agent. He can be an anti-Castro Cuban. He can be anything they want him to be as long as they don't tell you what he is really all about.

But, if you look at his life, he's an outcast. Here was a kid that had a 'kick me' sign on his back. Here was a kid they shunned in elementary school. I mean, you feel sorry for him because there are a lot of people out there that end up like this, and this is how he ended up. It's the driving motivation for him.

Throughout his young life Oswald thought he was smarter than what people gave him credit for, and frankly from a political standpoint, he was far better versed than anybody his age during that time period. But he was also mixed up emotionally and psychologically. If you want to find out about Oswald, look at his mother. She was the single most dominating force in his early life and so she helped form the attitudes he later carried.

But now flash forward to 1963. At the time of the shooting Oswald's closest friend is his wife, and he was separated from her. That tells you everything you need to know. Oswald never let anyone get really close to him. So the idea that somebody could get him involved in a plot to kill Kennedy wittingly, that is hire him, is impossible to imagine because Oswald's personality was not the type that would allow that to happen either wittingly or unwittingly.

Even George DeMorenschildt, who wrote a manuscript about Oswald years later, defending his friend Lee, didn't even know that Oswald attempted to assassinate General Edwin Walker. So, here's Oswald's only other supposed friend who didn't even know what he was up to that night in April of '63. So the idea that Oswald would be involved with confederates, who would manipulate him into doing something that he wanted to do, or force him to do something he didn't, seems to be rubbish. It doesn't sync up with his personality.

Now, on the other hand, I always thought that if there was a place to look for a conspiracy it was in Mexico City. Many books have covered that or tip toed around it, but the problem is that you will notice that a lot of them are hell bent on blaming this on the CIA. So, they end up getting blinded to the idea that there is a flip to that proposition and one that is much more likely in my opinion.

To believe that Oswald was being manipulated by the CIA, and they were using him, and meeting with him, and covering it up, makes no sense. I think what's far more likely is that when Oswald was in Mexico City and attempted to get a visa in order to go to Cuba and join Castro's revolution, he met with far more leftists and pro-Castro Cubans than has ever been exposed. There are quite a few conspiracy-minded people beating a drum today to get the CIA to release its files on Mexico City in the belief that they will tell us what really happened. I think what you really need is for the Cuban government to release their files on what they know about Mexico City, and of course the Mexican police at that time were in the pocket of Fidel Castro, so we need to get their files released as well.

Now, the things that went on Mexico City, we only know a little tip of the iceberg about it. My gut feeling is, if there is a conspiracy – and that's a big "if" — if someone aided and embedded Oswald, I think it was nothing more than this — that while he was down there, somebody, be it pro-Castro Cubans or pro-Castro Mexicans, winked and nudged Oswald, telling him that if he shot Kennedy that would get him into Cuba in a heartbeat. Something along the lines of, "You do that and get down here, then we will help you get into Cuba, and you will be a hero."

I believe that could have happened because Oswald supposedly shot his mouth off about wanting to seek revenge for Castro by shooting Kennedy, and of course those reports were immediately discredited by the conspiracy crowd because those allegations came from CIA intelligence circles. For some reason conspiracy folks are eager to believe the Cubans when Castro says he didn't have anything to do with it, but our own CIA, well they couldn't possibly embrace the idea of their innocence.

Look, it all goes back to Oswald's personality. What's more likely in light of Oswald's contacts? Is it more likely that his left-wing persona is all a lie, and he's actually a CIA agent who got framed, or is it more likely that what really happened down there is exactly what a life time of evidence indicates?

He was rebuked. He wasn't going to get a visa overnight. It was going to take months for him to get into Cuba. He then pulled some punches and went to some Cuban universities down there and a few gatherings. He talked with various leftists, some of whom probably offered to help him get a visa, but couldn't. So, he comes back to Dallas with his tail tucked between his legs and then two days before the assassination, on Wednesday, when it's announced that the motorcade route in Dallas is going to pass right by the Texas School Book Depository, Oswald realized his destiny was sealed. He knew then what he would do. He had told his brother years before, when he was living in Russia, that he had learned to always take advantage of an opportunity when it presented itself.

Now, fast forward to 1963. The presidential motorcade is going to drive right past the building in which Oswald works. It was like divine intervention, and he decided, I believe, to take that opportunity and act on it. He goes out to the house in Irving to retrieve the rifle. He asks Marina to move back in with him. When she says *No*, although she later admitted she just wanted to play him a little bit, that sealed Kennedy's fate. The fact that Marina wouldn't get back with Oswald led him to believe that he had nothing left.

Finally, getting back to the kid who was ticked his whole life, who thought he was smarter than anyone gave him credit for, says, *I'm somebody who's going to be reckoned with, and I'm going to prove it to you.* That's what he did. He took that rifle and he proved that he was somebody to be reckoned with.

Do you have any advice for future researchers when it comes to studying the case?

Yeah, do something else. (Laughs)

No, I shouldn't say that because I have enjoyed every minute of investigating this case, and I'm actually enjoying our talk now because it's rare that people actually ask intelligent questions, and as you can tell I can go on and on about this case. I remember years ago I heard someone say that if you study one subject for 45 minutes a day, in five years you will be the world's leading expert on that subject, whatever it is. At the time I first heard that I had already been studying the case for more than five years, and I was spending way more time than 45 minutes a day on it, so I don't know, maybe I'm a world expert, but how do you know?

But, to answer your question, I advise people to focus on the facts, and to rely on primary sources. Don't rely on secondary sources. That means you won't read my book or anyone else's book without looking at its sources or footnotes. I mean if you ask anyone on the street, "Who killed Kennedy?" Everyone has an opinion. They will name who they think did it. Then you ask them the next question and this is the one they can't answer. How did they do it? What's the connection between the group you just mentioned and Oswald? They can't answer it. All those conspiracy theories fall apart because you can't connect Oswald with *anyone*, and that's not a coincidence.

The bottom line is if you're interested in finding the truth about the assassination start with good sources, and apply common sense and logic.

John McAdams

John McAdams is a political science professor, an ardent conspiracy debunker and the author of the book *JFK Assassination Logic: How to Think about Claims of Conspiracy*. He also runs one of the world's most extensive webpages on the assassination of President Kennedy (mcadams.posc.mu.edu).

I found Professor McAdams to be very informed on this case. He enjoys his research on a personal level, and he works hard at applying logic to any conspiracy theory that someone presents to him. Throughout this interview, Professor McAdams used various points to counter many of the conspiracy viewpoints. He asks if we are willing to accept that one insignificant man could have killed the leader of the free world, if that is indeed where the evidence leads us.

Simply put, this interview presents the case that is against the conspiracy story.

What is your area of expertise in the JFK assassination?

I've studied the assassination since 1992. I started these studies in the wake of the movie, *JFK*. I have built a website dedicated to the assassination, and have authored a book on the subject as well.

Why do you think so many people believe that there was a conspiracy in the JFK assassination?

The reason why people believe in a conspiracy is because they don't want to believe one insignificant man could bring down the leader of the free world. In other words, they want to believe that where there is a great effect (JFK being assassinated), there must also be a great cause (a big conspiracy), and in that, it's easy to go ahead and blame whomever you dislike, whether it be the Texas oil men, the CIA, the FBI, the Soviet Union or any other group.

Why has studying the assassination been important to you?

Well, I'm a debunker by temperament, and there's a lot to debunk when it comes to the theories of the Kennedy assassination.

Why do you think the lone nut theory has gained such credence in the main stream media?

For the most part, the main stream media has some level of sophistication to it. In the 1960s the media knew a bit about the CIA. By saying this, I don't mean that the media was covering the Kennedy assassination up. What I mean is that the media understood the CIA, and understood how fallible the CIA truly was. Because of this, the media understood that the CIA wasn't capable of pulling something off like a presidential assassination. Thus, the media does not see much weight in the conspiracy theories, at least not enough to pursue.

Why do you believe that Lee Harvey Oswald acted alone?

I really don't know, but I think his motive involved two important factors. The first one being that he always wanted to be an historically significant figure. The second is that he desperately wanted to be an important leftist activist as well, but he never could pull it off. He wrote letters to the Communist Party USA and to other communist groups, but wasn't ever seen as a real member of the leftist community. When he assassinated President Kennedy, Oswald saw the fulfillment of both of these fantasies.

I'm going to play the devil's advocate here. If there was a conspiracy in the assassination, who do you think it would involve?

It's difficult to say. Seeing how Oswald didn't have very many friends, I would think it would have to involve some left wing fanatics, but only a very small number of them, in a very small operation. It certainly didn't involve someone like Cuba or the Soviet Union.

What do you think of the testimony of Officer Smith? (He claims he encountered a man who flashed credentials at him on the grassy knoll, immediately after the assassination.)

There was a lot of confusion following the assassination. Officer Smith thought the man who flashed credentials at him was a Secret Service agent, but many other people also mistakenly thought there were Secret Service agents around the area as well. These people were mistaken, because the Secret Service had no one on the ground at Dealey Plaza at that time.

Marilyn Sitzman is an example of this confusion. She was a witness of the assassination who claimed that Secret Service members got out of a car immediately following the initial shooting. However, these people she saw jump out of the car were most likely press members, so she was confused in her identification.

Also, it's important to remember that media members were all around the Dealey plaza area immediately following the assassination, and could have been mistaken as Secret Service agents due to the fact that the media wore jackets and ties just like the Secret Service did in 1963.

But, do you believe Officer Smith was telling the truth in his testimony?

I have no reason to doubt he *believed* what he said in his testimony. Remember, he said the man he thought was a Secret Service agent "saw me coming and showed me who he was." Unless Smith snuck up on the fellow, the "agent" just flashed something from a distance, and Smith assumed it was Secret Service credentials.

What about the testimony of witness Sam Holland?

Sam Holland was standing on the overpass during the assassination. He claimed that he thought a shot came from the picket fence on the grassy knoll, and that he saw a puff of smoke come from that area as well. He also claimed that after the assassination he went behind the picket fence and saw footprints and cigarette butts in the mud.

However, I believe that he could have been mistaken in his

perspective. I say this because Dealey Plaza is an echo chamber, meaning it was difficult for any witness to tell exactly where the shots came from. Also, the smoke he saw was probably the exhaust coming from the police escort motorcycles in the president's motorcade.

Saying that, I also understand Mr. Holland saw the cigarette butts, and footprints, but there was no other evidence of any shooter being behind the fence at the time of the assassination, so that testimony does not mean there was a conspiracy that involved a second shooter.

I see, but do you not think that Mr. Holland's testimony is worthy of consideration?

There is a point of overwhelming significance that psychologists raise when it comes to eye witness testimony. If someone says they see something, and they claim that they have no doubt about what they saw, they probably believe it. However, the accuracy of eye witness testimony is generally questionable, and that applies to the testimony of Sam Holland.

What about Jack Ruby? You don't honestly believe he murdered Lee Oswald out of compassion for Jackie Kennedy?

It's important to understand that Jack Ruby wasn't the sharpest tool in the shed. District Attorney Henry Wade said that it wouldn't be necessary for Jackie to come back to Dallas and testify in a murder trial but Ruby probably didn't know that. So that was one of several things that was in his mind. Some of the other statements Jack Ruby made reveal things about his motives. Statements such as, "I did this to show the world that Jews have guts," and Ruby telling the police that he did it because they couldn't, reveal that Ruby acted impulsively and possibly for self-aggrandizement.

A lot of researchers within the JFK assassination field tend to take shots at one another for their beliefs on the case, why do you think it's that way?

The pro-conspiracy people want others to believe there was a conspiracy, thinking that if you can get enough people to believe in a conspiracy then this will apply pressure to certain groups, and the conspirators will be revealed because of that pressure. An example of something similar is the global warming panic that's going on today. If enough people get worried about global warming it will supposedly get action. Thus, if anyone in the JFK assassination research field says that a conspiracy theory isn't true, and Oswald acted alone, then they are seen as obstructing justice and halting the pursuit of the true assassins. I believe this where the conflict comes from.

What advice can you give future researchers?

That they draw their conclusions from primary sources, and don't make conclusions based on a certain theory they heard about. Simply put, don't discover a theory and then try and fit sources into that theory so it will sound plausible. If you do that, you can make almost any conspiracy theory ring true. Follow the evidence, not the theory.

Do you think there is a place for logic when it comes to conspiracies?

Sure, the IRS conspired against conservatives recently, and I believe it's clear Abraham Lincoln was killed through a conspiracy. However, there is evidence behind those theories.

Why do you think the government has been so unwilling to release certain files pertaining to the Kennedy assassination?

The government has a record of keeping things secret. Bureaucrats are often unwilling to release any information on themselves because they fear their failures will be exposed, and they will be seen as incompetent. However, the government has released millions of files on the Kennedy assassination, and despite all the research into those files, there has been no smoking gun found. If anything, you would have to strain your eyes to see evidence of conspiracy through those released files. Therefore, it's my opinion that the remaining files that have yet to be released may be due to government institutions protecting themselves from being seen as inadequate.

Why do you think so many people don't believe in the magic bullet theory?

They haven't actually studied the evidence. Rather, they believe things they are told by conspiracy theorists, such that the bullet would have to zig and zag to hit both Kennedy and Connally where they were hit.

Max Holland

Max Holland is a well known journalist and author of the book, The Kennedy Assassination Tapes: *The White House Conversations of Lyndon B. Johnson Regarding the Assassination, the Warren Commission, and the Aftermath.* He is also a controversial figure within the JFK research community due to his views on the first shot that rang out in Dealey Plaza.

What separates Mr. Holland is that he believes the first shot struck a pole in the plaza, causing it to miss the presidential limousine. Other researchers believe the first shot missed and disintegrated on the pavement. Mr. Holland also argues, as most lone gunman advocates do, that the single bullet theory is the only possible conclusion that explains President Kennedy's and Governor Connally's wounds, minus the fatal head shot.

Despite the controversy, I found this interview to be a challenge to the conspiracy crowd. Mr. Holland raises good points about the physical and circumstantial evidence against the accused assassin, Lee Harvey Oswald. Either way, there is much to be learned from this interview.

What is your area of expertise in the JFK assassination?

Well, I wrote one book about Lyndon Johnson's tape recordings. I've written several articles for different publications, *Newsweek*, *The Nation*, *American Heritage*; newspapers, *The New York Times*, *Washington Post*.

Could you briefly explain what your theory is about the assassination?

I'm a believer in the Warren Report's bottom line accuracy that Oswald killed the President, and there's no evidence of a conspiracy.

What made you come to that conclusion?

Well, everybody has their own way of deciding what the truth is and I've talked to a lot of people who served on the Warren Commission. I've talked to many of the witnesses, from Oswald's brother to people in Dealey Plaza. I've read a lot of books, and that's how I came to my conclusion.

Why do you think that so many people believe in a conspiracy?

I think it goes back to the fact that Oswald didn't have a trial. If you look at Sirhan Sirhan, there's people who believe in a conspiracy there but for most Americans the fact that he had a trial and was found guilty put the matter to rest. With Oswald there never was a trial and that rightfully made a lot of people very suspicious. You know, why was he killed before he could have a trial? I think that's the basic reason. And then after that you start running into people with political points of view, and people who want to make money. But the basic reason is that there was no trial.

Could you understand why some people might look at the Kennedy assassination and see a conspiracy?

Sure. I don't have any problem with that. You know, it's probably a great place to start. Be skeptical. But that's a little different than not being accepting of rational evidence.

If there was a conspiracy, and it came out as so and was a proven fact- where would you think that would be?

I would suppose people putting up Oswald to do it, but there's no evidence of that.

Do you think the scientific evidence against Oswald is strong in this case?

Yeah, it couldn't be much stronger unless you had a picture of him firing the rifle. But, short of that it's just about as strong as it could be.

It was his rifle that was fired. He brought it to work that day. No one can account for where he was at the time of the assassination. He was the only person who fled the building after the assassination. He killed a policeman. I mean, how much more do you want?

I want you to know I do believe in a conspiracy, but I do not agree that everything in this case is a "set up." In light of that, do you think it's kind of a cop out to say that any evidence that leans towards Oswald's guilt is simply apart of the "he was set up" theory?

Well, yeah, if you say that you have an excuse for everything. You can use that to dismiss everything so that's the last resort for people who want to believe in a conspiracy despite the facts.

Could you briefly explain your work on the lost bullet theory?

Early on there was the perception that three shots were fired and each of the shots had hit either the president or Governor Connally. That was what life magazine had reported when they got control of the Zapruder film. That was what the FBI reported to the Warren Commission.

And then the Warren Commission came along and realized that Governor Connally and the president had been shot so close together in time, so that you couldn't work the rifle bolt that quickly. So they were faced with a problem. Either there were two shooters, shooting independently at almost the same time, or else the bullet had gone through the President and hit governor Connally, and the latter is what they decided was the truth.

So if three shots were still fired, that means one of them had to miss. The Warren Commission naturally were wanting to prove beyond a reasonable doubt that it happened to the two shots that actually hit and killed the President and they were much less worried about the shot that missed. So, when they put out their report they actually didn't have a clear understanding of what happened to the shot that missed.

Their explanation of the shooting sequence is very complicated as a result because they said if the first shot was the one that missed then this is what happened. If it was the second one then this happened. If it's the third one this happened. So it's a very confusing explanation and a lot of the critics sort of pounced on that to level criticism of the Warren Commission, and sometimes they misrepresent what the Warren Commission actually said.

But, in any case is was a vulnerability in the case that critics exploited.

Now as time went on there was more clarification of this. CBS, when it re-analyzed the assassination in 1967, was the first to say that it was the first shot that missed, and subsequently all the major investigations, the house committee, the book by Posner, the book by Bugliosi - they all agreed it was the first shot that missed. Their view was that all three shots had occurred when Zapruder was filming the motorcade, and I realized that was an assumption that wasn't necessarily true.

In fact, I don't believe it is true, and if you look at Zapruder's own testimony he knows he was suppose to hear three shots, but he says he actually only heard two, and I think he only filmed two. So I think the first shot occurred just before he restarted his camera, and that if all this is true it, explains why the first shot missed and that Oswald had much more time to carry out the shooting sequence than was previously believed. And it was not a difficult feat of marksmanship; it was pretty ordinary for an ex-marine with his training.

So you believe Oswald's time frame for the shooing was seconds instead of six or seven seconds?

Oh, definitely. No way it was six or seven seconds. It think it was slightly in excess of 11.

I want to focus on the witnesses in Dealey Plaza. When you have witnesses such as Sam Holland, who thought there was a shot coming from the grassy knoll area, or Officer Smith, who encountered a man claiming to be a secret service agent on the knoll immediately following the shooting, do you think those testimonies lean towards a conspiracy? On my behalf, I don't think we can just ignore these testimonies to make a certain theory fit.

Well, most of the time when you have a murder you don't have so many eye witnesses. You know, you're lucky to have a handful. And I'm not going to pretend I'm an experienced investigator of murders, because I'm not. But the fact is that when you have so many people, hundreds, witnessing an event, you're going to get a dispersion of accounts.

I mean it's an old trick in law school that law professors who teach criminal law do. They have a class where they have actors commit a crime in front of the class and he asks the students later what they remember, and everybody's account is slightly different, and I think that is obviously true here. You're not going to get one account. If everybody's account were the same, that would be cause for concern because people aren't tape recorders.

I mean, there was one witness who saw that the President and Mrs. Kennedy had a toy poodle in the car. So, you have to take the totality of the evidence. I agree with you that you can't ignore what's inconvenient, and in fact one of the reasons I came to my conclusion about the first shot was I felt some statements had been ignored because they didn't fit with the belief that all the shots were on the film. So, I agree with you there.

Sometimes the outlier is remembering something that's extremely important. But it comes down to your judgement and the preponderance of evidence. You know, most people heard three shots. Some heard two. Some hear four. Some thought they heard six. But most people heard three, and there were three shells found on the floor, so what are you going to conclude? That he picked up one of the shells? No, I think it's reasonable, given the totality of the evidence, that he did fire three.

You know, people say you can't cherry pick witnesses, but you have to be discerning. You know one person can say nine out of ten things wrong, and remember one thing that's an important clue. They also can remember nine out of ten things right and say one thing that is not true, so you have to exercise judgement and take all the evidence into account, including what people saw, what they heard, what the scientific evidence is, what the Zapruder film shows, what it doesn't show, what the other films show and you have to weight everything in and sift through statements. Then hopefully you reach a close approximation of the truth.

You know it's very easy to say, 'this person said this and so it's true.' You have to put what they said in the context of everything else too. Frankly, there is no physical evidence of shots from any place except where Oswald was.

I want to ask you specifically about the false Secret Service agent on the knoll that Officer Smith encountered. What do you make of that testimony?

Well, the Secret Service has said they didn't have any agents on the knoll, and unless you have proof to the contrary, then I just can't accept that that person saw a Secret Service agent there. Even if he did, so what? What does that mean? Is he saying that the Secret Service was complicit in the assassination, or there was a gunman on the knoll?

Well, I don't think they look at it like that. I think what they (the conspiracy researchers) are saying is that there was somebody impersonating a Secret Service agent on the knoll in order to avoid any detection from the police. What do you think of that?

You know, I heard it, I weighed it, and in the end I decided there's no value. It doesn't change the fact that Oswald fired all the shots and there's nobody else that I know of who did.

Why wasn't Bill Newman, one of the closest eye witnesses to the assassination, called to testify before the Warren Commission or the House Select Committee on Assassinations?

They couldn't call everybody and they didn't even interview all the Secret Service agents who were on the back follow-up car, and as opposed to Bill Newman, who wasn't expecting to see an assassination, these men were trained to be observant and to react. They didn't even interview all eight of them. The only one who was called to testify was Clint Hill because he jumped on the car. But the others had very important information, and they weren't called. So before I called Bill Newman, I would have called the seven others who were in that car. At least the three others who were on the running board and the two who were in the back. By their reactions you could have understood that something happened before Zapruder started his camera.

So, there were lots of people who weren't called. Bill Newman was interviewed and he was on television and it was right in front of him, but there are lots of people they didn't call, and there's a lot of people I would have called before I necessarily would have worried about him. Bill Newman, to his credit, has stuck to his story and I respect him for that.

I want bring up someone else who has been consistent in their story. I want to bring up Dr. McClelland who worked on President Kennedy at Parkland Hospital right after the assassination. Dr. McClelland says he saw a wound in the back of President Kennedy's head. Now I don't think it's good enough to write him off either, but what do you make of what he saw?

Well, I think a lot of that could have been cleared up if an autopsy could have been done as it should have been done first of all in Dallas, but even if it wasn't done in Dallas, it should have been done by doctors who were given time to do a proper job. Instead they were pressured to get it over with as quickly as possible because the widow was standing outside the car, and grieving. So, I think in President

Kennedy's case you have an irregular autopsy that came to the right conclusions, but through short cuts.

For example, when they wanted to dissect the president's neck because they saw the wound in the back and they wanted to trace the path of the bullet, they were denied permission because they didn't want the body disfigured anymore than it was, which was pretty silly in regards to what had already happened to him. So they were denied that and the first explanation was that the bullet had pierced his upper back and had fallen out backwards, which is ludicrous. And of course the next day when they talked to the attending physicians they realized the tracheotomy had been done over a wound. That's when they realized a bullet had passed through the president, so they wrote a report to reflect that.

All of that to say there are inconsistencies between the initial reports of the doctors who didn't really have time to examine the president, and between the people who performed the autopsy. You know the whole thing lasted about eight hours, four of which was given over to the funeral directors to make the body presentable for an open casket. So they did the autopsy in four hours and probably should have had at least eight. So you know there were issues that came because there was no protocol of doing a medical examination of a president who had been assassinated.

The government was not prepared. They didn't have experts on call. They let the feelings of the widow and the attorney general intrude on a strictly medical process. So you have these points of controversy, and I don't doubt Dr. McClelland, in the sense that he's telling the truth as he knows it, but at the end of the day, I don't think it's disputable that the bullet hit the president in the head and came out near the top of his head and was fired from the rear. So whether it was two inches below the cow lick, or two inches above the cow lick, it really doesn't matter that much, because it came from the rear and the only person who could have caused it was Oswald. So, while it's unfortunate that there was this discrepancy, in the end I don't think it changes anything.

As far as John Connally's testimony that he never believed that the same shot that hit JFK had also struck him, do you think he was honest, yet mistaken in his belief?

That's a good way of putting it. I did interview his wife once, and it's pretty clear to me that Connally wanted his own bullet. He wanted to believe he was a target too. He didn't want to accept that he was collateral damage. If you don't believe the bullet that passed through President Kennedy hit him, then give me an explanation of where it went. A real magic bullet would have been a bullet that hit President Kennedy in the back, exited his throat and then didn't hit Governor Connally. That would have been a magic bullet.

So you're saying the only place that the bullet could have gone after exiting President Kennedy's throat was into Connally's back.

Right. If you're going to say it didn't, you're going to have to give me an alternate explanation other than it disappeared into thin air.

Why is the magic bullet theory so disputed?

Well, first of all the initial presentation of the facts was that each bullet that Oswald had fired had found a target. Kennedy, then Connally, then Kennedy again. And so, the so-called magic bullet was at odds with that. It really was the only contribution that the Warren Commission made to the initial set of facts as we understood them, and people who were looking to criticize the report (thought) that it was a soft spot. How could one bullet do all of these things?

But when you look at, as I said, if you don't believe it hit Connally then you're going to have to give me an explanation of where it went after it exited President Kennedy's throat. This is military style ammunition; fully jacketed bullets in keeping with the Geneva Convention, which means they're made not to explode inside a person's body, which could cause a lot of damage. They're made so that with one shot you could maybe injure two or three soldiers.

Because that bullet was jacketed and made to travel through people, why is the head shot so violent in its exit wound compared with the exit wound found in President Kennedy's throat?

It goes back to hydraulic pressure. Most of the head is liquid. It's water and whatever else is up there. Very light matter in your brain. Most of it is kind of floating in liquid up there. Hydraulic pressure is tremendously powerful. If you pierce a skull with a projectile like that, you set up a tremendous hydraulic pressure inside the brain that's going to explode in the most violent way imaginable. When we were doing testing for my theory on the first shot, we were firing at these two-inch steel poles in order to replicate the traffic arm. One of our shots hit it directly and pierced a two-inch steel pipe. One of the shots we fired from the Mannlicher-Carcano was from 70 feet and it pierced it, so this bullet had tremendous penetration power.

One reason President Kennedy's reactions are so different is that one bullet hit him and essentially went through soft tissues and didn't hit any vital or major organs, and the other hit him in a place where it set up tremendous pressure. I don't have any problem saying that if you hit someone in two different places, you're going to get two different reactions.

Who was Lee Harvey Oswald to you?

He had just turned 24 and he was highly political. I would call him a sort of sociopath in the sense that he was very alienated from society and his family. He was thinking that the communist society was the better alternative to American capitalism. I think he was not well educated, but intelligent. He taught himself Russian, and read quite a bit. He was a frustrated sort of man. He was enamored with the Cuban revolution and Castro, and he read left wing publications and realized that President Kennedy was going to be driving by where he worked.

He had grandiose visions of himself and his role in world history. He interpreted that to mean, here was his chance to make a statement for the world about his views. I believe he knew we were trying to knock off Castro, which we were, and so he thought it was fair to try and knock off President Kennedy, and he did.

Could you explain Oswald's strange activity in New Orleans?

Well, one of my good friends is Yohan Rush who was a cameraman in New Orleans at the time, and filmed those scenes of Oswald handing out those handbills, and he has his own views on Oswald, but he definitely believes that incident was in keeping with his general political outlook. Mr. Rush talked with Oswald. No one was forcing him to start a Fair Play for Cuba chapter. That was what he genuinely what he believed.

He was very upset when he went to Mexico and the Cubans didn't recognize him as the revolutionary activist that he thought he was. If he had gotten into Cuba I don't think he would have killed President Kennedy. You know, he was always searching for a new place that was his idea of the better life, and Cuba was it at the time. So, I don't think there is anything inconsistent about his behavior in New Orleans at all. There's the radio interview he gave afterwards, which I think is very revealing of his attitudes about Castro and communism in general.

What about the Silvia Odio incident? I don't think she can just be brushed aside, do you?

I agree with you. It's one of those things that has to be taken seriously. However, I think it's probably just a case of mistaken identity. You know, there were a lot of people after the assassination who thought they had seen Oswald do this or do that, and that's one of the more prominent ones because it suggests involvement with persons, you know a conspiracy, behind Oswald.

But, to start out with, she had her dates wrong. Then she revised her account when she came to understand that Oswald could not have been there when she thought he was. So, I don't doubt she was visited by three men, I just don't think one of them was Oswald. I mean if you look at his whole behavior, here's a very ordinary person who didn't work well with people. Most of his life he was a loner and did things alone. He's not a cooperative type, and I just don't think he was there that night.

Now, was she visited by three men? Yeah, I'm prepared to believe that. I'm just not prepared to believe it was Oswald. Even if that did happen, and I don't think it did, it still quite a ways away from saying that anyone helped Oswald do what he did. Because even if you do believe that story, where does it lead? Well, one could say they believe Oswald was involved in this pro-Castro or anti-Castro activity because he was an intelligence agent in his own mind, but how do you connect those men to Dealey Plaza? I see no evidence they were connected.

What do you make of all the controversy involved with Oswald's Mexico City trip?

I wish there were an answer for every single thing. To me it's a mystery that nobody knows what Oswald did that whole weekend before the assassination. He didn't go home that weekend to visit Marina like he usually did; you know, what did he do? I've never read anybody who has a good explanation of what he did those 48 hours, and you think it's kind of important because it's the last weekend before the assassination. That would be the time he would be visiting with his co-conspirators.

But my point is that there are unsatisfactory answers for some things, such as, why didn't they have a photo of Oswald in Mexico when they had photo surveillance? I can understand them making a mistake, since they rushed that photo up not knowing who it was, but there's unresolved answers to things. You know, you have to go back a little in time. Oswald wasn't as important before November 22nd as he was after.

Why did the CIA repeatedly stonewall JFK investigations, and why do they continue to do so today?

Well, you have to look at it a little from the CIA's point of view. From their point of view, the cold war was far from over during these investigations. You have to remember that this was 1977-78. The Cubans that the CIA had been using, and were still using up until 2015 when we decided to normalize relations, were and still are alive. These are intelligence sources and methods, and to have investigators mucking around was intolerable. So they put George Joannides, who had been involved in 1963 with some of these Cubans and knew the lay of the land, in the position of a liaison. Yes, it's true that they didn't tell Robert Blakey who he was. Now, if that's outrageous and a lie — they felt they had interests that needed protecting from some of these investigators.

Okay. Let's say Oswald did have connections to the CIA, and they had nothing to do with his actions that November day. Is it in their character to never let that connection surface?

That's a little difficult to answer because I can't think of any precedence where he was connected. You know, the CIA really feels it's only responsible to the president in the office at the time. It's not a legislative agency. It's a little different now, but you have to go back to the way it was then. In those days the CIA was considered, and in fact was, an agency of the executive branch and in particular the president's intelligence agency and covert action arm. So, it was responsive to him.

If people from Congress asked it questions, if they could tell them the truth they would, but if they didn't have to in order to protect secrets, they wouldn't.

Now, has it ever engaged in such a cover up? Not to my knowledge. If it came out that somehow they had tried to engage Oswald and he was apart of an effort and after he killed the president it looked terrible, that would be a cover up. But the fact is, that is exactly what the FBI did. They covered up that Oswald had paid a visit to their office before the assassination. They lied about that. So are you asking me would the CIA lie about using Oswald? I say it's not inconceivable, but the fact is

I see no evidence that they did use him. Everything he did since coming back to the United States was consistent with his political beliefs.

You know, he fancied himself a sort of intelligence type operative, but it was in his own mind. No one asked him to do those things. He did them out of his own political beliefs.

What happened to President Kennedy on November 22, 1963?

Well, he came to Dallas, which was the only big city that voted for Nixon in 1960. He wanted the motorcade against the wishes of some there who were afraid of an incident because Dallas was known for being very conservative, or even right wing. The route was published a couple of days before in the Dallas newspapers. It turned out it was driving by the Texas School Book Depository where Oswald worked.

There was tremendous concern over an incident from the right wing, so the FBI didn't think Oswald posed a threat to the President, and as far as they knew he had never been violent. So, they weren't thinking of anything happening from the left, they were concerned about the right.

So, then Oswald, acting alone, killed the president.

I don't think he had much thought about what he would do, but he managed to get out of the building. When he was stopped by a policeman, he killed him, and then he professed to not know what the fuss was all about after he was arrested. That's what I mean when I said he was a sociopath. I think had he had a trial, he would have eventually talked, but who knows. He could have been like Timothy McVeigh and stayed quiet until the end.

What advice do you have for future researchers?

I think the best advice I have is to keep an open mind because discoveries can still be made. I myself made one I think is important because I was willing to entertain different voices, so I wouldn't stop learning. It's a great way to learn about human nature. You can see how people will stick to something despite the facts. So, I think the whole thing is a great way to study human behavior.

Secondly, to me it's no longer about the who did it and how and why. To me it's now about us, meaning, why does it invoke so much criticism and doubt?

Judge John R. Tunheim

Judge John R. Tunheim is a United States District Court Judge. In 1994, after the release of Oliver Stone's hit movie *JFK*, the public wanted our government to immediately release all remaining reports relating to the assassination. This demand for transparency helped birth the Assassination Records Review Board, which was created for the collection of all records relating to the assassination of President Kennedy.

Judge Tunheim was the chairman of this board. He was personally involved in the release of around five million pages of documents, and has seen the inner workings of what the government knew about JFK's murder. I loved interviewing Judge Tunheim because he brings a legal viewpoint to this case. He likes to shape his views on this case through the evidence that can stick in court, and this provides the reader with a good foundation to spring from.

I chose to place this interview in the Lone Assassin section because I would not call Mr. Tunheim a conspiracy theorist. However, he does admit that there are gaping holes in previous investigations of the president's murder, and he calls for our government to be more transparent about what they have hidden away. Let's take an inside look at what a judge's verdict would look like in this case.

Could you please explain how you were involved with the Assassination Records Review Board?

Certainly. I was nominated by President Clinton to serve on the Board, which was a five member decision-making board. We were confirmed by the Senate and took office in the spring of 1994 and we wrapped up our work at the end of September, 1998. We oversaw the review of records that agencies still wanted classified. We made decisions as to what should remain classified and what should be released. We gathered as many records as we could get access to that might even be remotely related to the Kennedy assassination.

Do you feel that it was an overall success?

I think it was a great success, due in part to the manner in which the statute was written. It was written with an eye to open as many records as possible. It was also due in part to the time in which we were able to work. The Cold War was over, so there was less concern about protecting old information, and it was before 9/11, so that the concern for protecting information to fight terrorism hadn't yet become a frontal assault on everyone like it did in 2001.

I felt it was a good time to release records. The way the statue was written was helpful because we were really the only outside group ever given authority to declassify records. That typically is reserved for the agency itself under presidential policies. Another factor in our success was very strong support from President Clinton. He had the ability to reverse any of our decisions to release information. He chose never to reverse any of our decisions. In fact, he affirmed our decision-making throughout the process.

And I think we had a fairly strong staff, and a good board that focused really on getting as much open as we possibly could. So, all those factors are why I think the work was relatively successful. I think somewhere between five and six million pages are now available to anyone at the National Archives.

Why do you think people have such a hard time either believing in a conspiracy or believing that Oswald did it alone?

It's a really good question. I think there are a number of different answers. One is the fact that this was in 1963. Investigations, at least initially, were not very professionally done. You know, we would almost laugh today at the thought that someone accused of killing the president would be paraded out in front of the press for short news conferences, or that the accused person would sit in a jail cell that was readily accessible by reporters wandering around the police station.

This was a different time in America, and I think that for starters we don't trust the investigations of that era, and secondly, frankly speaking, the investigations of that era weren't as thorough as they should have been in light of the gravity of the crime that had been charged. I think the fact that the Dallas police couldn't keep Oswald alive for more than 44 hours after the assassination only supports this idea of conspiracy.

As we look back at those black and white footages from the time, we think they just weren't very good back then. Even 20, 25 years later, investigatory standards had improved so much that when we looked backed we thought the local investigation must have been real shoddy. So, that's one reason. The second reason is people are prone to believe a plausible conspiracy theory. They're not going to believe wacky conspiracy theories that don't make any sense. No one is going to believe that the aliens came down to kill Kennedy. But, if there's a plausible theory, and plausibility goes along with the poor investigation at the time, people are willing to believe it.

President Kennedy was the most powerful person in the world, and the thought that he could be killed by a 24 year old misfit during a parade is not very believable to people. Therefore, the idea that there was a conspiracy behind it appeals to the mind and especially to people who want to learn more about the assassination. They want to look behind everything and see if they can see more.

Thirdly, I think there's another reason which probably lends more support to the idea of a conspiracy of some sort, and that is the fact Oswald had a fairly murky life in the several years before the assassination. He was in New Orleans and was associating with some unsavory characters there. He was involved in a pro-Castro effort at a time when our government was trying to kill Castro. He made a strange trip to Mexico City, where he went to the Soviet embassy and also the Cuban embassy. He had associations with people there. I think that there are tentacles there that lead people to believe that Oswald had connections with people who might have wanted Kennedy killed.

That being said, there's no hard evidence for that at all; all we have is the murky lifestyle of a misfit who wanted the world to think he was an important person. And so, I think those connections lead people to think he must have had some kind of tie in with organized crime via Jack Ruby, or maybe there's something to this Cuba connection, or maybe there's a connection with the Soviet Embassy in Mexico City. So, there are a lot of these tentacles going out from Oswald, and his life that caused people to believe that he must have been involved in a conspiracy.

I've said, you know, I'm a judge. I look at hard evidence. I look at what's provable in court, and the only evidence that's provable in court is that Oswald fired the rifle and killed him that day and that he had no involvement with anyone else That doesn't mean it's entirely true, but it does mean that is what is provable in court today, and that's why I say that about the evidence...because there isn't any direct evidence, at least that is admissible in a court of law, that would suggest any involvement with anybody else.

I have heard it speculated that if a group like the Mafia or the CIA wanted to commit a murder and applied a conspiracy to do it, that it's next to impossible to prove that conspiracy in court. Could you shed some light on that because of your legal expertise?

Well, I think contrary to what most people believe, it is not all that difficult to prove that someone engaged in a conspiracy. The legal standards in federal court, and in most states make it relatively easy to prove a conspiracy. You have to prove that the person that you're accusing of conspiracy joined in on an agreement, even if it wasn't really clear to everybody and even if it wasn't written down. There must be a meeting of the minds to do something and if you have evidence of that a conspiracy can be proven.

A conspiracy does not even need to be successful in order to be proven. For example, had Oswald lived and testified that he talked about assassinating the president with Jack Ruby ahead of time, and Jack Ruby seemed to agree that this was a good idea, then you've got a conspiracy. You could charge Ruby with murder of President Kennedy, even though obviously he was not there in Dealey Plaza that day. So, it's not too difficult to prove conspiracy. You have to prove a meeting of the minds, but it can be very informal. It can be merely through reactions of people or the discussions that they might have had.

So, it can be proven in court?

It can. If someone had actually come up with evidence of Oswald sitting down with one of the mob guys, one of Trafficante's guys or Rosselli's guys or something like that, and the subject of the assassination was discussed in advance, you at least would have the basis for a conspiracy charge, and maybe enough for a conviction depending on how persuasive the evidence was. You might even be able to connect the conspiracy to the mob leader if there's testimony that that person was aware of the conversation.

So, it's relatively easy to prove, but in this case you have no such evidence so we cannot even begin to try and prove it.

In light of that, is someone logical for believing in a conspiracy or for saying Oswald did it alone? Does it work both ways?

I think I probably fall somewhere in the middle, although obviously I believe, at least what the evidence shows right now, that Oswald did it alone. But, I never ruled out the possibility or the idea of a conspiracy. I just haven't seen sufficient evidence to prove that conspiracy yet. And, I say yet because there's still research being done that's solid, good research.

There's also sloppy research being done of course, that happens all the time, but there's good research being done too. The good research is trying to explore Oswald's connections to see if there were any that can be linked to the assassination.

Now, is it likely that 51 years after the fact we're going to uncover something major? Probably not. But, there are little pieces here and there that fill out the historical record. I would never discourage people from looking. My answer is it's always possible to uncover a fact which in light of later review proves something that you couldn't prove at the time, so I've never been discouraging to anyone who thinks there's a conspiracy and is hunting for it.

Having said that, I haven't seen the evidence yet that would prove that anyone but Oswald was directly involved.

On that note, the way the CIA has lied in this case and even obstructed justice in some investigations, can you see how people would think the CIA is suspicious, if not complicit in the assassination? Especially in light of the fact that they still have files related to Oswald in 2015?

I agree that the CIA's actions in refusing to release more records so many years after the fact is unfortunate. I mean, it violates not only the spirit of the law, but also the letter of this law, which is still in force. It requires agencies to declassify and release this information, and if we were still around they wouldn't be able to do that because we were able to exercise the power granted under the law to release a lot of material that the agency didn't want released.

I mean, I understand their thinking. They release something voluntarily and in their view that's precedent for some other issue down the line, so they're not going to release anything of significance. They do voluntarily through their historical review process routinely review old records from time to time to see what can be released.

Surely at the time the CIA was very much powerful, but also, as the Church Committee found, a somewhat rogue organization that acted above the law. The CIA didn't share anything with the Warren Commission. The Warren Commission was apparently not fully aware of Operation Mongoose, which was our effort to kill Castro, and destabilize Cuba, so I think it's understandable why people would be suspicious of the CIA.

But, you've got to look at the way the CIA operated at the time. They were rivals with the FBI in many respects. They just didn't feel that they had to follow restrictions. Today's CIA is much more subject to governmental control, of course, but they still do what they can to be secretive. One of these ways is to not release information that should have been released a long time ago. Even information about which they misled us back at the time when we should have known and we would have released it had we known the true story.

Why do you think they won't release those remaining files? What could possibly be the excuse for withholding those files now?

Well, there are two answers to those questions. The first one is embarrassment. They would be acknowledging that they flat out lied to the House Select Committee on Assassinations about George Joannides' role within the agency in the 1960s. And the second reason is about this precedent concern. If they release these files without being compelled to through years of litigation, then their view is that they will have 200 researchers at their door step saying, 'we want this information; release them just like this those files were just released,' and that would establish a precedent.

I think all situations can be distinguished. I don't think they would have the flood gates open like they think they would. But, I think it's shameful that they're not releasing it, and I can't believe that something so directly related to the assassination should still be protected today.

Is this type of behavior by the CIA not unconstitutional, and almost totalitarian state like?

They weren't exempt from the President John F. Kennedy Records Collection Act of 1992 which is what governed our work and which still remains on the books and requires agencies to identify assassination records and release them. The difference now is you don't have an aggressive board to force them to do it. We were there to force them to do it. The National Archives could try to exercise that authority and has chosen not to, so we don't have an agency pushing the CIA to release information and apparently the White House has decided this is beneath them and they're not going to push the CIA to do this either.

So, they're not above the law. There's no real enforcing mechanisms, so those who have been trying to sue for information are forced to use the Freedom of Information Act which is a traditional way to try and get government records. Under that law, it is difficult to get classified records from a federal agency. You know, it's not hard to get records from, for example, the Agriculture Department, but when you're going after intelligence records it's a lot harder to use the Freedom of Information Act to get to them. If you have a judge who is going to look at these issues carefully, you should be fine, but the CIA can be persuasive with its arguments concerning national security, especially in an age of terrorism.

The agency is not above the law; they have to follow the requirements for assassination records, but there's no one to force them to do it, and the Freedom of Information Act has been relatively ineffective.

What do you think of the work the Warren Commission did?

The Warren Commission did an exhaustive investigation. They had a good legal team and their investigators did a decent job. The FBI did some of the investigations for them, and history's judgment is that FBI investigators must have been tainted somewhat by Hoover's announcement the day after the assassination that Oswald had done it himself. Hoover was still running the FBI at that time with an iron hand of course.

The Warren Commission investigators did not have access to CIA intelligence information; that's fairly well proven, despite the fact that the former CIA Chief was a member of the Commission, Allen Dulles. Dulles apparently didn't reveal much that he knew about the CIA to the rest of the Commission. And Chief Justice Warren did not feel it was appropriate for anyone else to look at autopsy photos and X rays because they were relatively gruesome. So, those factors may have suggested an investigation that was not entirely complete.

You also have the Commission's single bullet theory, which is troubling to a lot of people, but certainly explained the evidence of what they found on the sixth floor and what they found from the timing of the shots and everything else from the Zapruder film.

I think, given the resources and information they had available to them at the time, it was a good investigation. It wasn't as complete as it should have been. And one thing we have to keep in mind about the Warren Commission is, it wasn't a special prosecutor, it wasn't a Watergate grand jury, it wasn't any of those things. It was a group of politicians chosen to oversee this investigation. And the reason why you have groups of politicians overseeing an investigation is to keep it under control.

I suspect part of the thinking was that if the evidence pointed to a foreign power, President Johnson wouldn't want the American people to know that because it would require retaliation and no one wanted that provocation at the height of the Cold War. So, by putting politicians in charge of this was a way to control it if it did come to the point being needed to be controlled. I don't think there was any need of control at the end.

I don't think anyone told the Warren Commission what to do. In theory it was a group that could have kept secrets that needed to be kept. So, overall they certainly don't get an A plus for their overall effort, but it was relatively exhaustive; maybe a B, I don't know. It's hard to say. 26 volumes and a lot of detail are fairly impressive when you look at the body of work that they created. I think the chief complaint about the Warren Commission over the years was that they were a group of politicians and they reached a result that a lot of people fundamentally disagreed with, and because they disagreed with their result that must mean they didn't do a good job, and I don't think that's a correlation you could make.

One of the most disturbing things about my generation and the way the law of the land is unfolding is that emotion seems to trump the law. I have run into this type of thinking a lot of the time while investigating this case. If you say Oswald has evidence against him, people will turn around and say that that evidence was planted. So, as someone who deals with evidence all the time, what would happen to these types of theories once they were in court?

The theories of someone putting a palm print on the gun and that sort of thing?

Yes, that Oswald was set up and that sort of thing.

Unless you had someone who directly testified that they were involved with doing that, there's not enough of an evidentiary basis or foundation to those theories to allow them to be admissible in court. I mean they're admissible in books written about the assassination, everything is, and it's an interesting theory and some people believe in it, but it's surely not admissible in court at this point, unless you find someone who was a part of the group and testified that they did this, and this is who we did it with, and this is where we did it and who had this role. No one has been able to find anyone like that, so although such evidence is not admissible in a legal proceeding, it is surely not inadmissible in the court of public opinion.

What about circumstantial evidence? Is there anything in this case that is circumstantial that would sway a jury towards conspiracy?

I hate to say never, because you never know. Juries can sometimes be swayed by outstanding lawyers and certain aspects of the evidence that's so persuasive to them that it overwhelms other evidence. I just don't see any evidence of a conspiracy that would be persuasive with a jury today.

Not to say that it doesn't exist out there, and that's why I always encourage people who are interested in the subject to look and to read and to think and to use their good sense to evaluate. And if you have the time and money to do investigations, then do it, because that's how we ultimately get to the bottom of the great questions of history. But, right now I don't see it.

I mean, civil court is different than criminal court. In criminal court you have to prove a defendant to be guilty beyond a reasonable doubt, which is a very high standard. In civil court you just have to prove a preponderance of evidence, which means it's more likely true than not. So, you're getting a little closer. If the evidence sways a jury 51 percent to 49 percent you've proven your case in civil court, so it's not out of the question, but from all of the stuff that I've seen it's hard to find evidence that's going to be persuasive to a randomly selected jury.

Do you think the American public will ever come to a conclusion on this case?

I think that the controversy will continue on probably forever in the annals of history. I don't think that you're going to firmly convince a majority of the American people that Oswald did it by himself. There's too much controversy about it. There are too many parts of the initial investigation that had gaps in it that can be filled with very plausible and interesting arguments that people can believe.

But maybe the controversy will diminish more at some point in time. You know, you still have people who are out there trying to prove that it wasn't John Wilkes Booth who killed Lincoln. They have other theories. So, you're going to find people who have a contrary view and this is especially true when they have been given their answers from the government, and that's their right as citizens.

Generally speaking, I applaud them. Go do it yourself. Figure out what you want to believe. But, there's so much here, so many books written that are contrary to the official conclusion, that I don't think that this controversy will diminish much in the next 100-150 years.

Do you have any advice for future researchers?

I think the most interesting part of research is to study Oswald. I think there are things we don't know about him. Assess him. Could he have pulled this off? Could he have met with people that made this suggestion to him? Did he come at this idea by chance because the parade route was going by the building where he worked and he was anxious to be a famous person in history? I mean, who knows? That's a place to look.

I would like to see more research done in the future on the Soviet Union's reaction to the assassination. Not that I think the Soviets had any role, but Oswald lived there for two and a half years before he came back in 1962, so who was he in touch with over there? What formulated his opinions over there? The KGB did an extensive investigation into the assassination. What did they find out? What's in their files? We haven't had much access into the KGB files or the Oswald surveillance files which are immense. Cuban intelligence. What did they know? Oswald supposedly had connections with Cuban intelligence officials when they were training in Minsk while he lived there. What about Mexico City? Mexico City has been looked at in some detail, but there is probably more to find there.

These are the kinds of in-depth research that I think have the possibility of shining a greater light on what happened, rather than continuing to debate over the single bullet or the sound wave analysis from the police motorcade tapes. Those areas have been tread over so many times, I'm not really sure we're going to gain any more information at this point in time. Let's look at Oswald. Let's look at his life and see what more we can find out.

So, start with Oswald and work your way out from him?

That's most interesting to me because you have all this evidence that he fired the shots on November 22, 1963, but the issue of why he would do something like this, what motivated him or who he was connected to, these are the issues that I find to be interesting and compelling, and still present open questions.

Gerald Posner

Gerald Posner, an investigative journalist, unleashed a title wave of debate about the JFK assassination when his book, *Case Closed*, was published. In his book, Mr. Posner came to the conclusion that Lee Harvey Oswald had acted alone in murdering President Kennedy. However, Mr. Posner didn't stop there. He also spent a portion of his time attempting to debunk conspiracy theories surrounding this case.

Whatever you may think of Mr. Posner, I believe his views on the case are important to understand. He focuses on Lee Harvey Oswald's past, and raises the question of how that past led him to the sixth floor window at the Texas School Book Depository on November 22, 1963.

What is your area of expertise in the JFK assassination?

Well, you know, I always think that nobody really is an 'expert.' All of us have spent time studying it, and different amounts of time studying it. So, if you just went by the time people spent studying it, the people looking at it for 30 years would be the experts. I don't necessarily think expertise should be measured just in terms of time. I think it's about weighing the evidence and coming to conclusions that you're willing to defend in a public forum.

So, I was always interested in the case. Jake, I was born in '54, so I was only in fourth grade when Kennedy was killed. When I went to high school and to college, it was still on people's minds and we all sort of felt it was a conspiracy. When I went to law school in '75-'78 the House Select Committee on Assassinations was taking place, so I was following it very closely.

You know, nobody goes into this case, any big historical case, with an absolutely clean "no opinion." What I mean by that is we all have some inkling about what we suspect happened. So, if you ask me about 9/11, I think it's 19 hijackers flying into the World Trade Center and the Pentagon. Somebody else might think it's the government or whatever. But you go into it with a supposition about what you think the historical truth is, and then you have to do your research and be open minded, and let the facts take you where they do.

In the Kennedy case, I thought it was most likely a conspiracy involving the Mafia. And the reason I felt the mob was involved was because of Jack Ruby. That murder of Oswald on that Sunday looked to me like a mob silencing, especially because Ruby had low level mob connections. So, I always was intrigued by the case, and I proposed it to a publisher who actually wanted to do a book that wasn't intended to solve it.

You know, you've been studying it. You did it right. You didn't want to put out something that just gave your opinion. I didn't think it could be solved. But, I had a different idea than your idea. My idea was to go ahead and examine the evidence. I knew everybody couldn't be right. One group thinks it's the mob; another thinks it's Castro; another thinks it's KGB; another thinks it's the CIA; another thinks it's renegade CIA agents like David Ferrie, and anti-Castro Cubans. Not everybody could be right, so I go in as a lawyer and investigative journalist, and see the five or six issues of this case that can't be resolved and say, '*here is a primer of the evidence in the JFK assassination,*' and identify each of the outstanding issues. You know, '*read this book before you read anything else in the case.*'

That was my idea, but the publisher wasn't interested. So, I went off and did a book called *Hitler's Children*. It was only after Oliver Stone did *JFK* that it took off. The only thing I have to thank Oliver Stone for was he sort of reinvigorated the JFK assassination in terms of the American public, and my publisher wanted to go ahead and have me do that book. It was only halfway through the research for that book that I realized that Oswald may have done it alone.

A lot of conspiracy authors have accused you of writing a book that is pro government. Are you a CIA agent?

(Laughs)

Obviously, I'm kidding…

I mean, I get it. President Kennedy was assassinated in 1963, and it was the perfect crime. They still haven't found these murderers right? They put it on this patsy, Oswald, and then, 30 years later, on the 30th anniversary, along comes this guy Posner who comes out with a book that says Oswald alone and all the mainstream press endorses him. He's got to be apart of the conspiracy; the cover up. So Posner must be working for the secret government or something.

Wow! I understand how that reasoning goes, but I got to tell you, it's so far fetched. That's why I laughed when you asked me that. Crazy stuff. It's America though. That's what makes us great. You can say things as a fact even if it's completely wrong.

One thing by the way, Trisha, my wife, does interviews with me on the books, and then she's involved in the editing and later she goes out on tours and she was with me when I was on that book tour. That was back in '93, when the book was published. We were in a radio station in San Francisco and I was on with Peter Dale Scott. He was with a woman, whose name I don't remember. She and Trisha were sitting on the side, off-air, and we were about to start the radio broadcast, and she asked Trisha, without kidding, what it felt like to work for the FBI. And Trisha thought she was joking at first, and she wasn't. She was serious. You know, I had to learn very quickly that that was an assumption from some people.

Do you discredit Silvia Odio because she suffered from emotional issues?

Put it this way, my perspective is that even if she didn't have any emotional problems, put all that aside, let's say she had been a Nobel Prize winning physicist. Whatever she was, there still has to be some evidence that links that incident to the plaza on November 22, 1963. To to say it differently, I'm open to what she says, but you have to come and prove it to me. That's what I always say.

But as of now, based on the evidence that exists, I can tell you without any doubt that Odio was wrong. And so, as to why she was wrong, I can't tell you. I did go on, and I did cite a number of reasons that I think effect her credibility, but I know factually she could not have seen Oswald that night.

Yes, but some researchers raise the point that she was either flat out lying about seeing Oswald, or at the very least someone was at her apartment using the name Leon Oswald. Could you make sense of that?

That's what I don't know. I'm not sure. That's her recollection, so was she right that somebody was using the name, Oswald? I don't know about that. If they were, then that is interesting because then you have to find out why they're out there using the name, Oswald.

Let's assume for a second there was someone there using that name. So, first of all, let's say you came out and you were able to produce a quality recording of that meeting she had with those people that night. It was long lost, and you had found it. And we find out the fact that it was just as she recalled. The guys introduced this man as Oswald. Then the question is, what does it mean? Does that have anything to do with the assassination? Are they trying to punk Oswald, or does it have something to do with setting him up regarding Cuban relations? Are they setting him up for something else?

So, even if that took place, I don't know if it has anything to do with the assassination. But, I'm not sure it took place, so the first question is did it happen? If it did, was it assassination related? Both of those are big one questions for me.

What do you think the CIA is withholding in their files that they don't want people to see?

You know, it's a great question because you can never figure it out. The CIA is its own worst enemy. They withhold files that often aren't critical or important to a topic because it relates to some other operation they had. But, in the end it's a big deal because it looks like they're hiding something about a murder. I get that.

The files in Mexico City are a total disaster. The question about whether they had audio tapes of Oswald, or whether they had a photo of him entering the Cuban or Russian missions, are ongoing. It's clear that the CIA had a cover up after the assassination. No doubt about it. They were lying to the Warren Commission because they didn't want the commission to discover the fact that they were in business with the Mafia to kill a head of state.

Many people in the Kennedy assassination think they were in with the Mafia to kill a head of state. They were. They were trying to kill Castro, and they failed half a dozen times or more. They never even got close. Of course, these same guys were supposedly the perfect murderers in Dallas, doing the same job that never even wounded Fidel Castro in Cuba.

But that aside, there's no doubt that they were lying and peddling backwards. I don't know if we will ever find out everything about Mexico City as a result. Files were destroyed. In addition, one of the reasons I say that they so hurt the search for truth is that when you withhold material for decades like they have, when you fight the release of it, every bit of it, all the time; when you don't disclose to the House Select Committee that the go-between the agency and the select committee was a guy who actually had ties to an anti-Castro group in South Florida, you cause people to be suspicious, and you hurt the process of discovering all the facts.

I mean, look, I get it. I wrote a book and it's called *Case Closed* and that's an arrogant title. I understand that. It doesn't have a question mark at the end. And because it's *Case Closed* and concludes that Oswald did it alone, and because when I'm on any program I argue very energetically, people assume that I'm therefore in lockstep and must agree with everything the government does, or everything they believe about the case, and I'm not open to any new inspiration.

In fact, I'm a very big critic of a lot of the things the government does, especially about what you're talking about here in regards to the CIA's documents.

Do you think Oswald may have mingled with some Cubans down in Mexico City?

I always thought it was possible. Mexico City is one the great question marks. Here's the key though. Let's assume that Oswald goes to

Mexico City. In Mexico City, there are only a couple of things that can happen. If he's applying to go to Cuba in the Cuban and Soviet Missions and that's sincere, and it's not a big operation, and you assume that Cuba and Russia aren't involved in a plot to kill Kennedy, their rejection of him sort of takes place on its own. If they had agreed to let him go to Cuba, he would have been in Havana when Kennedy was in Dallas. It means Oswald wouldn't have been there on November 22, and they would have had to get someone else for the assassination.

So, when he gets turned down, at that moment, let's assume he gets brought into a plot. They think he's susceptible to it and they urge him to join a plot. Then he comes back to America. At that point, I want one scrap of evidence that shows how the conspirators contacted him after he returned to Dallas, how they brought him into the active plot to kill Kennedy. Because he doesn't get the job at the Book depository for a while and the motorcade route is only released just days before the murder. So, you can't bring him in to the plot telepathically. You can't do it with a wireless message. It would have had to have been in person or by the telephone.

As opposed to Mexico City, where he's alone for while, he's now in Dallas in a rooming house with other guys who were all interviewed afterwards. You know, he went to see Marina on the weekends. So, I'm looking for the one visit from someone we don't know. I'm looking for that one telephone call that can't be explained away; the meeting at the depository or something with a stranger. If you present that evidence to me, I'm willing to change my mind and look at it. No matter what you believe about Mexico City, even if you lean towards the biggest conspiracy with him down there; when he comes back to Dallas he's still not into the plot.

As someone who is a lone gunman advocate, do you blame people for thinking there was a conspiracy to murder President Kennedy?

Oh, not at all. As a matter of fact, I think there are plenty of good reasons to believe in a conspiracy. Okay, if you study it in detail, I think the answer is that Oswald did it alone, but there is so much that happened here.

Even though I believe that the bullet that hit both Kennedy and Connally needs no magic, most people don't know that. They just look at that shot and think it's a magic bullet. You've got Ruby killing

Oswald two days after the assassination. How could you not think that something was fishy? You've got the assassin shooting at the president from a long range with a high-powered rifle, which makes us all think of a professional hired assassin. He then get's away in the immediate aftermath of the shooting and then his rifle is found with his fingerprints on it and your first thought is that he couldn't have been that bright to have killed the president and then leave the rifle with fingerprints at the scene.

So, I get it. Included with all that is we live a country where the government increasingly lies to us about everything from Vietnam to Iran Contra to Watergate. We know there are real conspiracies out there that happen. So, I'm not at all surprised that people think it's a conspiracy.

Let's say there was a big conspiracy involving the James Angleton's of the world, you would never find it written down on paper would you?

Yes and no. I mean, you'd be surprised what people put on paper. There are two different views of government here. You either think they are like James Bond, and everything they do is great, or I like to think of it as almost like the Keystone Cops at times. They can be inefficient.

That doesn't mean they can't do bad things. It doesn't mean they can't do things against our best interest at times. But, they can do really stupid things as well. They did put on paper some of those disasters with coups in other countries. So, I would not be surprised if the James Angletons of the world had proposed a plot like this, and put it down on paper somewhere. Maybe that's just my hope.

Why was the CIA so deceitful about Oswald in Mexico City?

I don't know. That's a great question. You know, long ago I gave up trying to second guess the motivation of why the CIA refuses to give over documents, because it's impossible to know in their convoluted byzantine mind what it is they think is so important about that. I wish I knew, and I do think that if history keeps going by we'll get those answers. I'm sure it's for idiotic reasons. I just don't know for which idiotic reason it happened.

I spoke with Dr. McClelland, who operated on President Kennedy and believes he saw a wound in the back of the president's head. He disagrees with researchers like yourself who say that he was mistaken in what he saw. What do you make of that?

I understand. There's no question in my mind that he is wrong, and I also believe he believes what he is saying. So, when people come out years later with a version of events, there's a thing called flashbulb memory. This is an important concept for you, or anyone investigating a historical case to remember. So, flashbulb memory is when an event takes place and it's a traumatic public event, and our memory works like a flashbulb in that event. Over time, our memory gets away from the event, and we try to fill in the blank spots of that memory of what happened.

With the Kennedy assassination, you can read about it instead of trying to fill that in with old memories. You can talk to other people about it. You can think about it afterward and fill it in. So, our memory can fill in the gaps with those types of sources. Do you remember when the Challenger space shuttle blew up? There was a study when people took a group of student's right after the event and asked them where they were when they heard about it, and who told them about it, and what time did it happen? So they answered those three things, and the people who originally asked the questions went back three years later and a majority of those witnesses ended up telling one or more of those three things differently.

The interesting part, Jake, is when they were shown their original statements they were convinced that their later statements were correct, and they must have been mistaken about what they had originally said. So, what's interesting about memory is that the new memory may seem more real to you than the original memory. So, I have no doubt that he's telling it as he remembers it, but I also have no doubt, based on the X-ray photos and autopsy pictures - and I know there are people who believe they were faked - but I'm convinced they weren't faked, that he was mistaken.

Even if Kennedy had been turned over in the emergency room; even if they had all examined the rear wound and every one of those doctors said the wound was in the cerebellum; I would say that that is just the eyewitness testimony. Now, is there better evidence than the eyewitness testimony? In this case there is. It's the photos and the x-rays. If those eyewitnesses contradict it, I would tell you they were wrong or mistaken.

What advice would you give future researchers when they're approaching a case like this?

Okay, go into it with your own feeling about what happened. Research it, and ask yourself questions, but be open to being persuaded by what you consider to be credible evidence. So, always be open to the evidence. You know, you reach a conclusion based upon what you have found and what you view as credible. As a journalist, you always have to be open to anything else that comes forward, and if you are going to research something, it doesn't mean you're going to answer 100 percent of all the questions out there.

That's what I would tell any future researcher. Don't come into this case and say "I know everything." All you can do is answer what is the most reasonable likelihood of what happened on November 22, 1963.

I think Oswald alone shot Kennedy. That's what I believe happened. I'm sure of it and for my sake, I'm confident that's what happened. But, will anybody be 100 percent sure of it? No, because you can't answer every question about this case to everyone's satisfaction.

Why should people today study the JFK assassination?

This case is the mother of all conspiracy theories. It's the original that started us off on a whole belief about what the government can do against us. I also think it's worth looking at because it shows how far you can take something that's history and turn it into entertainment.

Let's say you were a talented movie director, and tomorrow you came out and said you were making a movie about how the Holocaust wasn't real, or the Civil Rights movement never happened. I guarantee you the next day there would be demonstrators out in front of your studio protesting your movie because it is an abomination of history.

When *JFK* was made by Oliver Stone, there wasn't any protest like that. There were some reporters or columnists who wrote that they thought it was bad history, but there was no public protest of any sort. And that's because the Kennedy assassination has passed into entertainment. It's like a board game, 'Who killed Kennedy?' That's unfortunate.

My view is it was the death of president. We should be upset by a lot of the mangling of issues and facts in any given area of this case. I think it's an important case to study because it shows how history can be mangled, and you have to be careful when studying it. It's hard for the average person to tell what really happened, and what didn't.

Gerald Posner comments on this last statement:

"I didn't mean to imply that it was hard as a matter of ultimate fact to determine what or what did not happen. I think it is possible, just tough for the casual observer."

Gus Russo

As a veteran investigative reporter, Gus Russo brings an experienced eye to the often overlooked details of the Kennedy assassination. Mr. Russo has written two books on the Kennedy assassination, *Live by the Sword: The Secret War Against Castro and the Death of JFK* and *Brothers in Arms: The Kennedys, The Castros, and the Politics of Murder.*

I chose to place Mr. Russo in the Lone Assassin section because, for the most part, he believes Oswald was the only gunman responsible for President Kennedy's murder. However, he also believes that Lee Harvey Oswald may have had contact with certain Cuban intelligence agents in Mexico City, shortly before he allegedly assassinated the President of the United States. The Cuban aspect of this case is rarely ever touched upon, and I wondered why after hearing from Mr. Russo.

There are huge question marks about who Lee Oswald was with in Mexico City, and why the CIA worked so hard to ignore any evidence that pointed towards Cuba's involvement. Did Lee Harvey Oswald, who at least acted like he supported Castro publicly, murder JFK on behalf of Fidel Castro? If so, how much did Castro know about it? Does Cuba still have files on the JFK assassination, and if so, what are they hiding? Let's take a trip down the rabbit hole, shall we?

What is your expertise in the Kennedy research field?

Well, first I came out of college as a political science major. I had some ability to understand documents and politics, and my expertise in this case comes mostly from just being in the field and doing it. I was an amateur when I started. I spent a lot of time just interviewing people, and I learned how to acquire documents through the Freedom of Information Act. I learned how to use the National Archives and other institutions. But, it was just on my own basically, learning how to do it.

There's no school you can go to really to learn how to study the Kennedy assassination; you have to figure it out the very often hard way and expensive way. I wasted a lot of money on bad leads. I traveled to a lot of places that were a total waste of time. But, by doing that so long you get better at it - hopefully. I've done it since the mid-seventies, so that's my expertise, I guess.

Would you say that you focus on the Cuban theory more than most, or do you want to clear that up? Do you believe Cuba was involved?

I'm glad you asked, because that's been widely misrepresented. My conclusion is this, and I'm one hundred percent about it. I have no doubt at this point in my life. Oswald did it, He did it by himself.

He told people in Mexico he was going to do it in order to impress the Cubans in Mexico. He wanted to be a spy his whole life, especially for Cuba, and he went and did it. They encouraged him to do it. It wasn't like when people say that I believe in the Cuban angle; it's not that simple. The Cubans just encouraged him once he offered to do it. They didn't hire him. Castro didn't hire him.

I see people say on the Internet, "Russo says Castro did it." No, I don't say that. Oswald did it. Castro's people became aware of what Oswald was going to do, and looked the other way to a degree, they certainly didn't alert the Secret Service, and, from my sources, they encouraged him.

Now what that leads to is that when Lyndon Johnson learned of that, that's disastrous because the American people will conclude that Castro was behind it, and that would have led to a confrontation, a nuclear confrontation probably with Cuba's sponsor Russia like we almost had during the Cuban Missile Crisis.

So, that's what I believe. Oswald did it. The Cubans were aware he was going to try to do it. But that was enough to cause a cover up.

In your book, "Brothers in Arms," you do make the point that some of Castro's intelligence officers may have known Oswald before he went to Mexico City in 1963. Do you believe that these Cubans contacted Oswald to meet them in Mexico City?

He had written letters to the Cuban embassy in August of '63. I'm fairly certain he contacted the Cuban Embassy, letting them know he was going to arrive. It's unclear whether they ever received them or knew. He was certainly upset when he got there they didn't seem to be expecting him.

In August of '63 he told Marina, "You know, I'm so excited. We no longer have to highjack an airplane to Cuba. I found another way to get there, through Mexico City." And, it's possible I knew how he knew that, but I can't remember that right now. But, at some point he learned. Now, it could have been through his Cuban contacts because the sources we developed through the German film told us, a number of sources told us, that there was communication with Oswald all during '63.

Actually during late '62 through Mexico City, the Cubans were in touch with him, so they could have told him. Now, the fact that they were in touch with him shouldn't lead you to conclude that they were doing anything with the assassination. He was just trying to ingratiate himself with the Cubans, and say they'd hired him as a spy in America, but they, like every other government, didn't take him seriously. That's why he goes to Mexico, to convince them that he's the guy, because they weren't taking him seriously.

Now one of those contacts could have told him about the embassy in Mexico City, I'm not really certain of that.

For the sake of context, the G2 (Cuban intelligence) was pretty strong in America in the 60s. With Oswald handing out pro-Castro leaflets in New Orleans, would these Cubans have known about him, and his willingness to do impulsive things for the Castro government?

That's part of the reason, I think, they were wary of him. They knew he was impulsive and he did those things. As I said in my book, what we learned in our investigation was that the Cubans were made aware of Oswald the day he returned to America. He was here. They were aware of him because Vladimir Kryuchkov of the KGB sent his file to Havana when Oswald returned to America and said 'here's a guy you might want to have some contact with if you're looking for eyes and ears in America.'

So, we were told by a number of people, that they did reach out to him. They had people in New Orleans. They had people in Miami. They had people everywhere in the Cuban communities, and they reached out. We don't know the details of it, but we had enough good sources that we believe that contact was made with Oswald, and he didn't impress them, and that's what I believe had him frustrated.

I believe he shot at Walker, for instance, to impress the Cubans. He handed out the flyers to impress the Cubans. Everything he did that year was to establish bona fides with Cuban intelligence, but he couldn't do it. So, to get back to your question, they were well aware of him. We were told specifically that they were made aware of him by the Soviets.

Could you touch on the mystery of 544 Camp Street, and the leaflets that Oswald had printed there?

Oh sure. I practically lived there in the 90s; I was there so much. I was there last June as well. I went down there a lot, and spent a lot of time interviewing those who worked at Camp Street.

As far as the infiltration, in my first book, *Live by the Sword*, where you see a reproduction of Oswald's diary where he talks about how he's infiltrated the Cuban groups, and blah blah...that was what he was trying to do. He was trying to be a spy and infiltrate the anti-Castro movement. I spent a lot of time working on 544 Camp Street and this was a part of his agenda; to get into these Cuban groups. That also is what he wrote into his diary about how he's learned about their re-invasion plans for Cuba, and it sent him through the roof when he learned these kinds of things.

In my opinion, his agenda was he was trying to be a spy. He always fancied himself a spy from the time he was a child, and we all got immersed in the James Bond books in the early 60s, and Oswald did too, but he didn't have the goods and he didn't know that. You know, he's in New Orleans getting into all kinds of trouble. Things that the Cuban intelligence wouldn't sanction probably.

You know, there's a certain kind of tradecraft that all of these intelligence agencies have, and they don't have somebody running wild in the streets doing things that aren't under control of some kind of organization. So, that's what you have with Oswald. You have a guy who's sort of out of control; wants to be somebody, especially for Castro's organization, and nobody takes him or her seriously.

So, you can see things get ratcheted up, as he gets more frustrated. You know, he starts with shooting at Walker, and then he's handing out fliers, and getting on a radio show. These are things the Cubans probably never would have sanctioned. They would never allow one of their "spies" go on a radio show to do a debate. This is supposed to be undercover, you know, secret stuff.

Then he wants to highjack a plane, and it's crazy of him. You can see the frustration growing month by month. His life is falling apart. His marriage is falling apart. Nobody takes him seriously, and he was about to explode and that's exactly what happened.

Moving forward to Mexico City. Oswald goes down there and checks into a motel that's a Cuban intelligence hot spot. Am I correct about that?

That is correct.

So, when you see something like that does it not bring up the question of his previous contact that wanted him to check into that specific motel?

That's a great question. I don't think I've ever answered it or been able to approach it. It's one of those ones that, you know, I don't know if we will ever be able to answer. I would not be surprised if the people he was in touch with from New Orleans told him certain things about where to go when you get down there and where you can stay, and who to contact in the embassy and so forth. So, I wouldn't put it into a book because I don't know it. It's certainly reasonable, but I just don't know the answer to it.

Do you think a reasonable person could be suspicious of something deeper?

Sure, but that's different than saying, "Come down to Mexico, and stay here so we can talk about killing Kennedy." Killing Kennedy was not what this was about at that point. The conversation would have been more along the lines of, "okay you want to be a spy for Cuba then come down to Mexico to meet other spies here." I don't think for a second the Cubans said "Come down to Mexico, we'll tell you where to stay, and we will talk about killing Kennedy."

The Cuban agents we spoke to say they wouldn't for a minute think of hiring this guy for something like that. They thought he was as crazy as the Soviets and Americans did. That's one thing all the countries had in common. But when he goes down there and offers to do it saying, "I'm gonna do it anyway. I'm gonna take a shot. I'm gonna kill that bastard Kennedy," which was reportedly what he said inside the embassy. I think at that point they said, "Well he's gonna try, we might as well tell him he'll be a hero and encourage him. Maybe he will get lucky and do it, and the plots against Fidel will stop."

I think it all came from him. I don't want people to get the impression that the Cubans had contact with him and then told him about Mexico, that that had anything to do with killing Kennedy. I think that was more just business.

So you think it's possible that Oswald was going to fulfill his dream by possibly getting to talk to someone in the embassy, but he went a step further being the impulsive person he was?

Exactly. You know, he went down there to get a visa to go to Cuba. That's probably what they expected him to say when he went down there. Before he went down there he prepared for this. He brought his whole resume with him of all the "spying" he had done, in the streets agitating; all of the pro-Castro clippings; the radio debate, because he was trying to impress them with his spy craft. So he was upset when he went in and saw Silvia Duran and she wasn't expecting him. I mean, she didn't know who he was.

So, that leads me to believe that he thought they were expecting him. Bringing his resume, and all this stuff. That's part of the reason he got upset with her. But she hadn't been in touch with him; she didn't know who he was. And he said, "I thought you were expecting me? You don't know who I am? Here's my resume." All that kind of stuff. That wasn't the level of person in touch with him. She was as surprised as the next person.

Of course, in a few hours she was told who he was. But, that's where it comes from. It comes from him trying to make himself a spy, and go to Havana and work for the G2. They were never going to do that with him.

Let's say you have this connection with Oswald and Cuban intelligence in Mexico City, and the Cubans encourage him to kill Kennedy. If that is the case, then don't you have Cuba murdering the president?

Exactly. Exactly. That's different than saying Castro did it. You're right. The end result is the same. If the American people were allowed to know that Cuban spies were working with Oswald in Mexico City that would have been enough to start World War Three. That's what Johnson hears in his head. He says, "Oh my God, that's all we need. I don't care if you can't prove Castro ordered it. It doesn't matter." Once you show him meeting with Cubans, talking about killing Kennedy, it's over. That's the problem.

If that's the case, were we living in a world where President Johnson and company didn't really care enough about Kennedy to go after Castro? Was it better for the country not to? In my logic, you would want to bring people to justice even if that meant war. But, will you touch on why our government would cover up Oswald's dealing with the G2?

As far as the government covering it up, I don't think a lot of people in the government knew enough to cover anything up. This was tightly held. Johnson knew. A few other people knew what this meant. Robert Kennedy knew. It was a cover up by just a few people.

As far as whether Johnson cared for Kennedy, think logically at this point. Kennedy is dead. Johnson even said to Earl Warren when he was getting him to head the Warren Commission, "you know if you don't do this 40 million people could die," because he remembered World War One. He remembered how that war started with one leader in a car getting assassinated and then 20 million people are dead. It's a mess, and he remembered that, so if I were in his position I would have certainly cared about justice for Kennedy, but in a way they already had it because they got the guy who shot him. You know, they got Oswald. Oswald got killed. Now they have to say "okay is it worth finding out what Cubans knew what and jeopardize the lives of 20 or 30 million people when JFK was trying himself to murder Castro?"

You know, it's not like he's a saint. That's why I called my first book *Live by the Sword.* Live by the sword, die by the sword. Johnson had that in his mind. He felt like JFK had played a dangerous game. Kennedy started all this. The murder plots and the invasions against Castro. It's not like Cuba ever tried to invade America and Kennedy was just trying to get even. No, we started it, and I think Johnson looked at this picture and said, 'Kennedy brought all this on himself, now am I going to start World War Three to find out if any Cubans knew Oswald did it?' I would have done the same thing Johnson did. I don't think it's a question of, did he care for Kennedy. He saw Kennedy as the guy who was trying to murder somebody.

Do you believe President Johnson disagreed with JFK on his kill Castro policy?

Oh yeah. I spoke to so many of his aides and intel people. Look at what happened with the plots. When Kennedy dies, isn't it a great coincidence that the plots against Castro just stop in their tracks? That should prove right there that this wasn't all inspired by the CIA; the White House drove this.

And Johnson, there are quotes by him in my book, about how outraged he was, and how he stopped all this stuff instantly. And frankly, the CIA guys told me they were glad he stopped it. They didn't want to do it. So, this was driven by John and Robert Kennedy. It jeopardized the planet, and certainly the Western Hemisphere, but it was a pride thing for them. Johnson understood that, and I think a lot of people understood that in Washington.

Outside of Washington people didn't know this game that's going on. Kennedy was feeling embarrassment over the Bay of Pigs. This drove him and his brother crazy, and the CIA group were ordered to do what they were ordered to do. Many of them just shaking their heads and just wishing it would end because they knew it were dangerous.

Sam Halpern and all of those guys told me it was out of control. They had no idea why he was doing this; why he thought Castro needed to be killed. But, "we follow our orders. We work for the White House." The CIA is apart of the executive branch, and their boss is the president directly. That's how they do it. It wasn't their idea, believe me, and Johnson knew it. They were glad when he stopped it. That's what they told me. That's why Johnson is quoted as saying the Kennedy's had created a Murder Incorporated.

Look at all the quotes from LBJ in my first book where I line them all up where Johnson just says they got what they asked for. They played a murderous game, and Castro got him first. Those are Johnson's words. So, now it's over. Why push it any further?

Bouncing back to Mexico City for a little bit; could you describe the meetings Oswald had with the infamous "red haired" Cuban there?

Well, we learned one thing for sure. Red haired black men are not impossible or unique. They do exist, and they do exist in Cuba. To a person in America, they think, "Oh, there's no such thing." Well, you ask Cubans and they'll tell you different. There are red haired, dark skinned people, and there's a name for them. I write that in the book.

What we pushed further was we got into the files. The Mexicans did their own assassination investigation, which no one has ever seen except our team. The National Archives can't get a copy of it, but they exist. In their files there's a photo of the guy, and under his picture it's written in Spanish, uh, 'the red haired black man.' He existed. A number of people down there said, 'of course he existed.' CIA files talk about him with corroboration. So, we had no doubt when we came out of that that this was no joke that you just laugh at. The guy existed, and he was one of a number of people who was escorting Oswald around in Mexico City trying to figure him out.

You will never get a completely clear itinerary of that week, but it's safe to say a number of Cubans associated with the embassy were with Oswald outside of the embassy. They were well aware that they were being bugged. The Cubans knew the whole game. They knew they were bugged inside the embassy. They knew where the microphones were. They put a show on for the listeners. What we were told is that when they wanted to talk about something serious they would meet in other places, because they knew the game the CIA was playing. They were a step ahead of everything.

So, when Oswald comes in they put on a show for microphones, and they slip him a note that says, 'meet us at the restaurant at four o' clock,' you know, something the CIA can't hear. And then, the serious meetings take place outside the embassy, and the CIA knew this. They admit this. In fact, in my book I show pictures of the Cubans taking pictures of the CIA guys taking pictures of the Cuban embassy. It was all just a game that was played, and nothing serious happens in the embassy. It all happens in restaurants and bullfight arenas...wherever. You have to know how this game was played to appreciate what was going on.

Getting back to your question, the red haired Cuban did exist. A G2 officer named Oscar gave us his name in fact. He was one of the people who tried to debrief and figure out Lee Harvey Oswald. Again, not trying to hire him, just after Oswald goes into the embassy and talks about 'killing that bastard Kennedy,' they pull him aside and say 'let's talk.'

Then you have the infamous phone call from a worker in the embassy the day that Kennedy was shot. This phone call described how this woman knew about Kennedy being shot "almost before he did." This woman is also ecstatic and laughing about Kennedy being shot in the face. Can you elaborate on that?

Right. I believe it was the Luisa Calderon call. She was whisked out of Mexico City after the assassination. Yeah, she was one of the ones who were in touch with Oswald between his visit and the assassination seven weeks later. It was clear he was in touch with somebody in the embassy. There are records that show that.

You know, we've always been told that the transcript of her conversation, which was in the Warren Commission I believe or certainly in the HSCA, that she was just being sort of casual about her comment, and it was no big deal. But, I put a FOIA out and for those Mexico City tapes and got them released for the first time, and I sat down in the National Archives and listened to them and that's when we put them on the show. And you can hear, she's laughing. She is ecstatic that he's gotten killed. It's not just "Oh, he got killed, it's no big deal." They're in ecstasy over it, and you know, that's an important phone call. That's why it wasn't released much sooner to the public because it's inflammatory to hear the Cuban people in the embassy who knew Oswald, laughing about Kennedy's death and saying "knew almost before him." It's pretty serious stuff.

So, Oswald was in touch with a lot of people in that embassy, and some of them had foreknowledge that he was going to do something.

After the assassination, she and others were pulled back into Cuba, and now they're next to impossible to get a hold of?

Exactly. We couldn't get them. The House Select Committee was promised they were going to get to speak to Mrs. Calderon. When they got there, Castro said she was sick, and couldn't meet them. There are just a lot of people you're never going to get to meet in Cuba, who just know too much. So, that's been a problem. I would have loved to speak with her, but you just can't do it.

What about the woman who dealt with Oswald in the embassy, Silvia Duran? Do you think there is more to her? Did she have a romantic relationship with Oswald outside of the embassy?

Take a look at *Brothers in Arms* and you'll see that I interviewed a number of people in Mexico who confirmed a relationship, and hanging out with her at a dance party, and all that kind of stuff. Phil Shenon found a few more for his book. But, it's overwhelming to me. If fact, I interviewed June Cobb. She was there with the Durans and Elena Garro after the assassination - Garro saw Duran with Oswald at the party. She said it was crystal clear in her mind. Cobb was there when they were privately talking about it, not when they were talking to the government or investigators. She was in Garro's house; June Cobb was there when they were talking amongst themselves, saying "Oh my, that's the guy we saw at the party with Duran." They all knew it. So, it's too big to be a lie.

June Cobb I trust entirely and the other people we spoke to as well. So, yeah, I think she did have a fling with him. I'm not sure what it means eventually. I think she was ordered to keep an eye on him. To take him around. "He's a little nuts. We need somebody to be next to him. Just go out and have a good time with him." This is supposition here, but this makes the most sense to me. She gets involved with him to a degree that they have a sexual fling, and that's the end of it. I don't think she has anything to do with a plot to kill Kennedy.

You know, they have a thing in spying they call the "honey trap" or the "honeypot" where they use a beautiful woman to get what they need to know from people. It's done all the time, and I think that's exactly how she was working. Get next to this guy; find out what he's about. So, there you have it. Duran finds out, through her own contacts in the embassy, that there was more to this than just Oswald shooting Kennedy, because she told my producing partner Willy, "There was a complot and I'm gonna tell you about it."

Well, in the film you see Willy show up with his camera at her house; but, since then she's been warned. Since her first statement to us she's been frightened into not talking. She's changed her mind. She won't talk. That happened a lot down there. People wanted to talk but were frightened to death. Silvia Duran did tell us "there's more to this and I'll tell you if you come to my apartment." Willy went there, and she'd been frightened off. She wouldn't talk anymore. Not that she was involved in a plot, but she had been in the embassy and heard things.

So, that's it. It's not this huge, big plot where Silvia Duran is involved in the Kenney assassination or anything. I think she was a spy. Her good looks were used when people would come into the embassy that they wanted to get next to. She later learned that Oswald had made this boast that he was going to kill the president, and she almost told us on camera, but she changed her mind.

So, who does she fear in Mexico City? Why won't she talk?

Oh my God, well the atmosphere in Mexico City, you have to know this to understand this at all; the terror and fear that comes from the

Mexico City police is powerful down there. Willy would call me up, and say "Gus, they follow us constantly down here." He would say, "I'm on the phone here in a restaurant in Mexico City. The secret police are five feet away from me at the next table just staring at us". I mean, it is oppressive down there. It was the fear of death, and it's a very violent nation. You know, there are a lot of murders that go on down there, and the guy who started it all, Barrios, is key to understanding all this.

He was the one in charge of the secret police when they really put the fear and terror into people, especially with the Kennedy assassination. He was the one who interrogated Silvia Duran for the CIA Station Chief Winn Scott. The problem is, he was a great friend of Fidel Castro. His terror squads really did terrorize those people, so if you want to die or get hauled off and never be seen again, you talk to an American investigator about Kennedy and Oswald.

It's very fearful down there to this day. That's what people don't understand about this case. It's hard to break into Mexico City. I mean, look at the people we had on camera. Every single one of them wanted their faces obscured. None of them were paid anything. None of them volunteered to talk about this. We had to coax them over months and months. The Cuban embassy employees we put on camera, the security guards, the guys in the film who sat down, those guys weren't paid anything. They were frightened to death to talk. They said, "Please don't use our names. Don't use our faces. Here's what happened."

So, the fear is there. It's the same with Silvia Duran. It's the same with Gutierrez. You see in the film where Willy goes to the apartment of a witness who saw Oswald with the Cubans and he talks through the door to the family. They say he's living in fear. He's changed his name. He can't talk. That's pretty amazing, you know, 45, 50 years later that they're still that fearful, but they are. That says something about the Mexican secret police.

Could you touch on Gilberto Alvarado, and how he was involved in all of this? Was he credible?

Only because other sources that we believed told us things that they didn't even realize were corroborating his story. You know, pictures of the red headed Cuban and so forth. Those pictures exist. Oscar told us that Oswald hooked up with this guy. If you read Alvarado's interrogations really closely you'll see that, yes, he retracted because the interrogator started threatening to cut his balls off.

Then he retracted the retraction. That's common down there because of the fear that's put into anybody that knows about this. So, the last thing I think he ever said was that all of those retractions were out of fear.

Yes, it really happened. I really saw it. We tried to find Alvarado. We had a guy go down to South America and we found out that he had passed away. We really spent a lot of money, and we tried to find him. We found his family, and they said he had just passed away.

But, at any rate, I do believe him. His story is probably not 100 percent accurate. Nobody's really is. There are all kinds of exaggerations that come in over the years, but the essence of it is true. The other thing is you really don't even need it because we have so much more. We have so much information about Oswald in Mexico that you can throw Alvarado out if you want. You still have other people talking about the same exact thing. So, how much do you need to say there's a lot of smoke here? Well, apparently Lyndon Johnson had enough.

Do you believe Oswald received money from the Cuban intelligence?

Well, according to what Oscar told us, and I believe him, because he was very emphatic about it, he said Oswald was not about money. He was not being hired to do anything. It was all ideology for him. "We gave him just enough money to hang out in Mexico. We gave him basically walk around money. It wasn't money for the assassination. He didn't ask for it." So, yeah, Alvarado may have seen money getting exchanged, but it was nowhere near the amount he might have thought. Oscar made it very clear to us that this was not about money. He didn't need money to convince him to do anything. So, that's been misconstrued.

With all if this evidence, why is it so hard for people to even consider the Cuban theory in this case?

Well, that's a good question, and I may have an answer for it. I'm not sure. Now, full disclosure, I'm a liberal, lefty bleeding heart, but I have to tell you that if you look at the books that are written about the Kennedy assassination and look at the politics of those who write them, I bet it's 90-95 percent liberal people. The inclination is to say evil government, CIA, blah blah blah. It's the normal inclination from the left to blame the government.

I'm on the left myself so I see that. The problem is that's no way to write a book of investigative journalism. If the books had been written by the right wing, which they're not, they don't care about the assassination for some reason, you would have had a whole different thing. They would not have been afraid to go after Fidel Castro.

The extreme left has always seen Castro as this romantic revolutionary, a wonderful guy. He's a hero to a lot of the left. They hate the thought of anybody like myself saying Castro's people may have been involved in this. He wasn't such a good guy after all. I mean, Oliver Stone, when he did *JFK*, he was given the idea to do *JFK* when he was in Cuba. Somebody handed him a book about Jim Garrison in an elevator. Do you think Oliver Stone is going to say Castro's people did this? He's not going to look in Mexico City.

That's the typical view from the left. They won't even look at that. It's organized crime, or the CIA, or the oil people. They don't even think about Castro, he's a great guy. But, that's wrong. I think somebody on the left should be able to admit that Castro, especially in the early 60s, was not a great guy. The G2 assassinated people all over the world. These are not good guys.

I mean it's amazing; Oswald is a guy who lived, breathed and died Castro, and it's like the elephant in the room, and yet it's the last thing people want to consider. I think it's because Castro is viewed as this romantic revolutionary, but nothing could be further from the truth. It's a sad thing.

Here we are talking about normalizing relations, which I'm for because those people have suffered enough, but I think why did we have these relations with Cuba over 50 years? It makes no sense economically or morally, because we have fine relations with Vietnam, who killed 58,000 Americans. When did Castro ever do that? We're fine with Vietnam. We're fine with China. What is it about Cuba that put this all into motion that we absolutely cannot have relations with them?

There's only one thing. They never came clean about what happened to JFK. I think the old timers who put all of these laws into the books about embargoing Cuba; these are the ones who believed this. In Washington circles, what we are talking about here, this Castro idea, is not unknown in Washington. It's outside of Washington that this is a crazy theory. In Washington, they all sort of lean that way. All of the people in Washington said if this has anything to do with anything, it's Cuba, and it frightened them to death.

So, for writers to not consider that, it blew my mind. I thought, "Am I crazy? Why has no one written this book?" It's right there. Khrushchev wrote that Fidel wanted to have a first strike nuclear attack on America during the missile crisis. That's how crazy he is. So, is this a guy who wanted get Kennedy killed, after Kennedy tried to murder him? Of course he would.

The biggest thing you can take away from this interview is that people who have these theories that Castro was a good guy or Oswald was a good guy, they don't know either of those people. They have to spend more time learning about those two characters than reading about E. Howard Hunt or Richard Helms. I mean Oswald was a horrific person. This not a guy you would like. To defend him for a microsecond is insanity. Oswald murdered people. He wanted to murder more. He shot at General Walker. He put a gun in Nick McDonald's nose, an inch from his face. He pulled the trigger; tried to blow is head off but the gun jammed. It would have been another person killed that day.

So, what I'm saying is, this is a horrible guy and you know, I feel bad for him in a way because an awful mother raised him. He had two strikes against him the day he was born; he was a diseased person and murderous. For a writer to say "I'm not going to spend more time learning about him, I'm going to spend time learning about some CIA officer" is lunacy. It's grasping at straws. The thing is staring at you right in the face. I traveled the world for Frontline. We spoke to everybody we could find. We spoke to hundreds of people who knew him; Marines who were with him; people who were with him in the orphanage; his childhood friends and his high school friends, everybody. We came away with understanding that he is, and that's what you have to do."

Okay, let's move to the aftermath of Dallas. Was there a plan to eliminate him or would they just roll the dice with him?

That's a good question. There are two things. If he gets caught alive, what's he going to say? Do you think for a second the Cubans in Mexico City gave Oswald their real names? He doesn't even know whom to name. He has no one to implicate. If anyone went down there they would say they never talked to him. He came in and screamed about a visa, you know, that's all we know. These guys are good at what they do. I'm sure they didn't give him names so they could implicate him in a courtroom, so that's number one. Secondly, we were also told that this plane that came into Dallas the day of the shooting that flew into Redbird airport and so forth, that although they promised Oswald help with escaping, what they really were going to do was kill him. If the police didn't kill him, they were going to kill him.

That isn't something I can come anywhere near proving. I think we only had one or two sources that didn't want to be named. People in Mexico told us the plan was that if he got away with this thing, we would have someone on the ground in Dallas to take him out. So, you're right, it's a fair question. They considered the fact that he might get arrested, and I think they were prepared to deal with it through fake names, and through killing him if they could.

If they would have killed him, wouldn't that have led to Cuban complicity? Didn't Jack Ruby do them the biggest favor in the world?

Oh, for sure. Yeah, a lot of people breathed a big sigh of relief when that happened.

So, it couldn't have worked out any better for them?

Absolutely. But, it couldn't have worked out any better for them because of the times. Cuba also knew that even if Lyndon Johnson thought we did it, what's he going to do? You know what I mean? If that's what they thought, they were 100 percent right. He was not going to start World War Three. This was not the era of mustard gas, and rifles and cannons. This was nuclear weapons. It would have been the first nuclear exchange. I think the Cubans knew they weren't going to start a war over this.

Lyndon Johnson knew Castro was behind it, in his mind. He said it a dozen times until his dying day. But, he told my friend Marty Underwood, who asked him about Castro, that he was not going to have his first act in office be to press a button and start World War Three. That isn't going to happen. So, he was acutely aware of all the innocent people who would die and I think Fidel Castro might have thought he would have thought that. So, there was a lot hanging in the balance. It wasn't a normal murder where one person gets killed and then you take the guy who did it and put him in jail. No. The world would have blown up, and you think differently when that's thrown on your shoulders. You know what I mean?

So, do you think Oswald missed his rendezvous with the guy he was supposed to meet afterward?

Yeah, I think that's a possibility. I think Cubans may have said, and to be clear this is complete speculation but it makes sense to me, we're gonna meet you at Redbird or somewhere. You can get a bus, go here, and we'll meet you and whisk you off to Havana, when they were just going to shoot him. In fact, now that I think of it, I remember the detail. We were told the plane was supposed to pick him up at Redbird and drop him over the Pacific Ocean. That's what it was. That's what the Cubans told us. Okay, so he's on his way to possibly meet Cubans, get a bus to go meet them, and it's all done in by JD Tippit, whom Oswald also murdered, forcing him to hide out in a movie theater, where he was caught. So, that's what we were told. They were going to dump him in the ocean.

Did Oswald have a bus ticket in his pocket?

I don't think he had a bus ticket, but he had enough money to buy a ticket. Warren Commission attorney David Belin was big into this. He was convinced that Oswald was going to get a bus to Mexico, and he looked at all the prices of the bus fees. He had just enough to get to the border, although I don't think he was going to go that far. I think he was going to an airstrip to meet these guys, and they were going to kill him, but JD Tippit and Jack Ruby…they thwarted the plan.

Are there still Cuban files, or Mexico City files out there that can shed some light on the assassination? Are we ever going to get to see these files?

Yeah, but I wouldn't get my hopes up. There are files in the archives in Mexico City. There are files in Cuba. There are KGB files that have never been released. They only released a fraction of what they got. We got more than most, because we had a source that got into their files and pulled stuff out that nobody's seen, and he only had a few minutes in with the material. There are files in a lot of places, but keep this in mind too - everything isn't written down. As a top CIA told me, people have this impression of files and paper. He said in their line of work the most important things aren't written down. That goes for every country. It's not like we are gonna get all these files, and everything is gonna be clear. Sam Halpern said, "You think we write this stuff down?"

The night of the assassination, Sam Halpern guaranteed me that Lyndon Johnson was on the phone to Mexico, talking to all his contacts down there. He knew the President of Mexico, who was the former head of intelligence. He had great contacts in Mexico, and based on what they told him, he made his decision.

Also, Sam told me, "the most important things that are written down aren't put in the filing system. If we have to give something to Lyndon Johnson, we hand deliver it, and you'll never see it again. You might get lucky, and find a few things to get written down and kept by accident, but a lot of it is just verbal." Al Haig told us that in his presence he saw Lyndon Johnson destroy files from Mexico City. He wrote about it in his memoir, but nobody read it. He was involved in the Cuba project with Robert Kennedy and the Pentagon right at the time it all happened. He was in the White House that weekend. He saw information about Cuba and Oswald be destroyed in his presence in the White House, and that file will never be seen.

You know, there weren't photocopies or anything. It was just that one copy. So, you know, the good copies get destroyed. The great stuff never gets written down. So you have to live with imperfections in history. You're never going to nail it completely down. But, I know enough. I'm happy with my knowledge now that I know enough to know why things happened. I understand why the cover up happened. I understand who Oswald was. I understand who Fidel was. I can move on from it. I don't have time to have every nut and bolt nailed down. No history is perfect; none of it is on any subject.

Why did the CIA destroy the photo's they had of Oswald in Mexico City, along with his voice recordings, and lie about it? Are Cubans in the picture with Oswald?

Well, yeah, I'm convinced that's what it is. I'm convinced that there are Cubans in the photos with him, and it would do the CIA no good to bring that out. Because the CIA is sensitive about this too. Had they been more proactive…they could be perceived as having screwed up in Mexico City. They had Oswald photographed with Cuban agents, and they had tape recordings, but they didn't put two and two together because Oswald wasn't on their radar as a violent guy. They didn't process these tapes until after the assassination.

You have to picture; they have dozens of tape recordings coming in, and literally have one person listening to them. So they are piling up in a room. They don't get listened to the day they are made. So, they are in a stack in a room with one secretary and translator and the stack doesn't get worked down for months. So, in the middle of that stack there's the recording of Oswald in the Cuban embassy, and after the assassination they realize they had those recordings and people didn't hear them. People are going to think they were negligent. So, they had to cover up their interests.

There is a lot of that going on in this with the CIA and the FBI that has nothing to do with who murdered President Kennedy. You'll see that with Oswald and his address book that has the page torn out of it by the FBI. That's an after the fact cover up. But, that has more to do with them covering their own interests. It's how Washington works when something happens. People are trying to keep their careers intact. It rarely has anything to do with a conspiracy; it's more just the way Washington works.

Some researchers believe that blaming Cuba was a disinformation campaign created by the CIA to shift the blame away from their complicity. What do you make of that?

Well, they ignore a lot of things, not just Oswald and the intelligence officers, but they're ignoring the fact that there's no evidence that anybody but Oswald shot Kennedy, and if that's the case they got a real problem because Oswald is linked to nobody outside of Cubans. He didn't have mob guys in his phone book. You know, so they ignore just mountains of evidence to place this at the blame of the CIA. One of the many things they're overlooking is that the CIA was very close with President Kennedy. They had a great relationship with JFK. He tripled their budget. His brother was at CIA headquarters most days after his work at the Justice Department. He was a hands on guy. He was running the CIA/Cuba stuff.

You know, the CIA did an internal study about their relationships with every president since the agency was formed, and said by far their best relationship was with President Kennedy. Okay, so what is their motive to kill him? There is none. My point is the conspiracy theorists tend to overlook everything.

Okay, just to be blunt. Did Cuba kill our president and get away with it?

My opinion is that Cuba allowed President Kennedy to die, and Fidel Castro was among those who knew what was going to happen. That's as far as you can go with it. You can definitely say that Cuba got away with it, and maybe that's why we sort of punish them by not having relations with them for 50 years. I don't know. It's the only thing we could do. So, yeah, at some point you have to decide your battles, and I think that's exactly what Johnson did. He said, 'I'll live to get them another day, and in another way we will find a way to even with Fidel or with Cuba or maybe we will just let God do it, but it just isn't worth it.'

What advice could you give future researchers?

I would say in general be very skeptical of everything you read. If you want to get into this don't trust any writers for yourself. Go first hand. Talk to the people who you think knows something first hand. I'm fortunate I live in Maryland and the whole government lives here. The FBI, Secret Service, they're my neighbors, and I can work into that world pretty easily. My dog walker friend is branch chief at NSA, so I know these people. They're not monsters. They're just people. Most of them are very good patriots. So, it's good to ask first hand questions to people in government.

I spent a lot of time and money going to New Orleans, talking to people who knew Oswald. I went to Dallas and spoke to everybody who knew these people, and if you do that, you can come up with a decent conclusion. But, before you do that, be very skeptical of all this stuff because people have agendas. They won't believe that I am one of the ones who didn't have an agenda, but I can't convince people of that. I really didn't. But, assume I did, and check me out for yourself. Talk to the people I have spoken with. See if I'm lying; see if I'm wrong. Think about human nature when you consider any case like this. What motivates people to do what they do? That includes Lee Harvey Oswald. That includes Fidel Castro. That includes John F. Kennedy. Their motivations were pretty obvious when you think about it.

Oswald was diseased. He was mentally ill. Kennedy was full of jealousies and retribution. That's they way they were brought up. Castro and he were privileged. That's why I spent so much time on their character in my books. Once you know who they are, everything starts to make sense. It's much more obvious than what people think. These are just people with the same motivations that everyone else has. It's not a big conspiracy. They hardly exist. Think of your own life. When have you ever seen a conspiracy that big? When have you ever seen two people get together and one didn't squeal? Name one conspiracy in all of history that has proven to be that big? It doesn't exist. It's not human nature. Do you know any ten people who could get together and do something like this? And, we are talking about hundreds of people in this.

Dave Phillips

In light of the talk about David Atlee Phillips, and his possible role in the JFK assassination, I wanted to give his son a chance to give his views on his father. Here is what he had to say.

You're not the first person to contact me, and my attempts at dialogue have left me with a bad taste in my mouth. The usual contact is from a conspiracy theorist who is looking to validate his theory, and who refuses to accept any fact that detracts from his intellectual package. You will have to do with a brief statement, and here it is.

My dad thought of life as an adventure, and I think his autobiography captures that side of him well. He was also a caring father, and a good and fair man in general. He admired John Kennedy and was appalled to have been named as part of the supposed assassination conspiracy. Like other CIA employees I grew up around, he didn't join to be part of a government mafia; they were there to continue serving the United States, the way they had during World War II. The weakness in their devotion was the quasi-military sense that they should do what the president ordered them to do, even when they thought it was the wrong course of action. Which is how one winds up with the Bay of Pigs, for example. But if you think about it, this devotion to the commander-in-chief is the polar opposite of the idea that the CIA would do in the commander-in-chief. If there was a conspiracy to do in John Kennedy, my guess would be that it was orchestrated by Havana. But my actual guess (nothing more) is that Oswald really did act on his own, after getting the polite brush-off from the Cubans. We'll never know until the Cuban intelligence files are declassified.

As for why my dad got tagged: for any horrible, incomprehensible act, there are those who make it comprehensible by turning to a conspiracy theory. (And what satisfaction there is in constructing a neat, tidy answer to something that had been so messy and disturbing.) The conspiracy theorists needed someone to hang the conspiracy on, and when my father retired and went public he inadvertently provided them with a target. Interesting how quick people are to defame someone they never met, and about whom they know nothing.

End of statement. Good luck with your book.

Dave Phillips

Get Involved

If you are interested in getting involved with this case, here are some basic tips to help you along your journey.

1. Read the books of the researchers I interviewed. They are all credible people, and you can pull a lot of information from their years of research.

2. Get involved with researching the government files of JFK's assassination. There are thousands of documents about JFK's murder that have already been released to the public, and they need to be studied with a disciplined eye. You can reach out to JFK experts such as Debra Conway or Bill Simpich to find out how you can dig into these documents today.

3. Be open minded. Don't lock into one theory or another simply because you prefer it. Be willing to learn from opposing viewpoints, and challenge yourself to keep growing in knowledge.

4. Don't get lost in social media groups. Social media has been great for this case, and it has also been a disaster. Just because someone runs a social media group on the assassination, does not mean they are an expert. Study who you are learning from before you study what you are learning from them.

5. Watch documentaries. There are a lot of good documentaries out there on the JFK assassination, and I think they are one of the fastest ways of getting acclimated to this case. For starters, I suggest any student watch the Frontline documentary, *Who was Lee Harvey Oswald?*

6. Pick up the phone and call greater minds. Don't be afraid to reach out to other researchers if you are stuck on a point. Be courteous to these people, and always remain respectful to any view they may present to you. It is not your job to debate them. It's your job to learn why they have come to their conclusions.

7. Push towards a final civilian panel. After all the remaining JFK files are released, and we go through their content, I believe we

should have a civilian panel write an updated report on JFK's assassination. Ask older researchers to get involved with this idea, and prepare yourself for service as well.

8. Visit Dealey Plaza. If you are going to investigate this case, you will need to take a trip to Dallas, Texas and visit the scene of the crime.

9. Talk to your younger friends about history. Ask them who they think killed President Kennedy, and then educate them on the different theories.

10. Don't let this case consume your life. I love to study the past, but I never allow it to take priority in my life. This case can be addicting, and some people have ruined their lives pursuing it. While I think getting to the bottom of this issue is important, I don't think it is above taking care of the people right in front of you. History matters, but your present history matters more.

Epilogue

No matter what you believe about this case, I hope you come away from reading this book with one perspective: It still matters.

As the flame over President Kennedy's grave flickers in Arlington National Cemetery, questions over his death still linger in our post-modern society. The interviews in this book have attempted to resolve a lot of those questions, but it will be up to individuals like yourself to pursue them further.

If you do choose to travel this path, you have no shortage of information available to you. There are years upon years of research out there that has been preserved by dedicated experts from previous generations. However, it will be up to our generation, and the next, to make sure this information doesn't silently pass away with time.

We must add to the sum of this knowledge by approaching this case through simple logic, and allowing ourselves to draw our own conclusions based on where the evidence takes us. That's why I believe this case should be approached through an apologetic-type format. What I mean is that we should ask future students to begin their research by debunking any theory they can through hard evidence. This was one of the goals of my book. I knew younger readers might be overwhelmed by the mass of information in this case. I didn't want them to get burnt by false theories, so I tried to ask questions in such a way that they could get involved through critical thinking. It's a simple formula that our generation loves to chew on: critical thinking leads to asking more questions, which leads to more research.

Another thing I encourage you to do is to speak up. Don't be afraid to raise a point about any topic in this case. Nobody knows everything about JFK's murder. As a matter of fact, we could use fresher minds that may be able to look at the facts of this case and draw out new perspectives. The old guard must be willing to allow new researchers to have an opinion, even as younger researchers should show appropriate respect for elder researchers.

Above all, we must all be willing to share and pass our information along to the next generation of researchers. I freely confess that I had a lot of help from my JFK elders in researching this book. I don't know where I would be without their insights. Yet, I also had to be teachable in order to learn from them. I decided early on that I would scratch all my preconceived ideas about JFK's murder, and that I would open my mind to hearing opposing viewpoints. I hope you will do the same.

I would caution against approaching the study of any aspect of history with a haughty spirit. History is never one-sided, so you cannot afford to be one-sided while you research it. It is my fervent hope you can benefit from this book, and that it stirs you to greater intrigue.

I've asked this question of the many experts I've interviewed for this book, and it seems appropriate to pose it to you:

Why does the Kennedy assassination matter today?

On November 22, 1963 the president of your country was murdered in broad daylight. He was a father, a son and a husband. Not yet 50, he was heading towards his second term in office. His heart beat with conviction, and his mind carried a vision for a greater world. All of this was lost to an assassin's bullet.

Our country has never fully recovered from that event. Why? Perhaps it's because we as a country don't believe this case was ever given an honest investigation. Today it is common to distrust our elected officials. Many of us are apathetic about politics, and perhaps with good reason. If I could point to a moment in American history that launched us on the path to our modern skepticism, it would be the Kennedy assassination.

I believe this is why it still matters today.

The debris of JFK's murder affects our current worldview, yet we act as if the modern world is immune to the dangers of ignoring history. We seem to believe that answering the questions of November 22, 1963 won't make our world a better place.

But ultimately, the truth matters. Perhaps that is one reason this case has captured the imagination of so many of our predecessors. They wanted to know the truth for the sake of settling the record. So should we.

As many of the researchers in this book pointed out, we are responsible to the call of history. It is both our right and obligation as citizens of this nation to keep demanding the full disclosure of the facts of JFK's assassination.

What generation has the permission of history to claim its past days have no impact on its present ones? Indeed, history matters even if we claim it doesn't. The effects of an uneducated generation are tragic because we become disarmed, unable to confront future events that may occur. What if the President of the United States were to be assassinated in our time? What if it was a conspiracy, and our government lied about it? What if uncovering the truth about that assassination would decide our immediate future?

How we would respond to such a catastrophic event hinges on our understanding our past. That is why President Kennedy's assassination matters. We have been called to keep history alive…before history dies.

People, Places & Things

John. F. Kennedy: The 35th President of the United States of America. He was the father of two children, Caroline and John Jr., and the husband of Jacqueline Bouvier Kennedy.

Lee Harvey Oswald: The alleged assassin of President John F. Kennedy. He was a former marine who attempted to defect to Russia, and returned to the United States afterward with a Russian bride. He was murdered by night club owner Jack Ruby.

Jack Ruby: A Dallas nightclub owner who murdered Lee Harvey Oswald on national television.

John Connally: The Governor of Texas who was wounded in the same attack with President Kennedy on November 22, 1963.

George de Mohrenschildt: A Russian émigré who befriended Lee Harvey Oswald after he came back to the United States from Russia.

General Edwin Walker: A highly decorated general who served in WWII and Korea, known for his ultra-conservative views. Targeted by an assassination attempt, allegedly by Lee Harvey Oswald, on April 10, 1963.

Lyndon B. Johnson: The 36th President of the United States. JFK's vice-president, he became president after Kennedy was assassinated.

J. Edgar Hoover: Long time Director of the FBI.

Robert Kennedy: Attorney General of the United States, and JFK's younger brother.

J. D. Tippit: A Dallas police officer who was murdered, allegedly by Lee Harvey Oswald, shortly after President Kennedy's assassination.

Marina Oswald: Lee Harvey Oswald's Russian wife.

Fidel Castro: Prime Minister and later President of Cuba.

Nikita Khrushchev: First Secretary of the Communist Party, Chairman of the Council of Ministers and Premier of the Soviet Union.

David Atlee Phillips: A CIA agent involved in covert actions against

Cuba. Allegedly the same "Maurice Bishop" who met with Oswald in Dallas shortly before the assassination of President Kennedy.

Antonio Veciana: An ardent anti-Castro militant, and the leader of the group called Alpha 66. He reportedly identified Lee Oswald with his former CIA case officer, Maurice Bishop in Dallas shortly before the assassination of President Kennedy. Veciana later identified Bishop as David Atlee Phillips.

Gaeton Fonzi: Former congressional investigator who worked for the House Select Committee on Assassinations. This committee was tasked with re-investigating President Kennedy's murder in 1976.

Ruth Paine: A Quaker who studied the Russian language and culture, she befriended Marina Oswald shortly before the assassination of President Kennedy.

George Joannides: A CIA officer who managed an anti-Castro group called the DRE. Joannides served as a liaison between the HSCA and the CIA.

James J. Angleton: Chief of Counterintelligence in the CIA.

Silvia Odio: A Cuban exile and member of the exile group Junta Revolucionaria Cubana (JURE).

Sylvia Duran: A secretary at the Cuban embassy during Oswald's visit. Allegedly romantically involved with Oswald.

Joseph Campisi: A Dallas restaurant owner with reputed organized crime connection. A friend of Jack Ruby, he visited Ruby in jail shortly after Oswald's murder.

Carlos Marcello: Known as The Godfather and The Little Man, Marcello, was an Italian-American Mafioso who became the boss of the New Orleans crime family during the 1940s. Allegedly threatened to have President Kennedy killed so that Robert Kennedy would stop his war on organized crime.

Jim Garrison: A District Attorney in New Orleans. He investigated the Kennedy assassination in the late 60s, and eventually charged a man named Clay Shaw for conspiring to murder JFK. Shaw was later acquitted. Garrison became the focal point of Oliver Stone's film, *JFK*.

The Texas School Book Depository: This is the building in Dealey Plaza where Oswald worked. Oswald allegedly fired three shots at President Kennedy from a sixth floor window in the Depository.

The Grassy Knoll: A grass-covered area in front of a stockade fence in Dealey Plaza. Assassination witnesses claim to have heard at least one shot fired from behind that fence.

The False Secret Service Officer: Dallas police officer Joe Smith encountered a man on the grassy knoll immediately following the shooting. This man flashed credentials that lead Smith to believe he was a Secret Service agent. The Secret Service claims it had no men on the ground at that time.

The Acoustics Evidence: An old Dictabelt recording, allegedly provided by a police officer who was riding his motorcycle in Dealey Plaza at the time of the shooting, containing the sound of gunfire. Acoustic experts claim there was a 95% chance that a shot did come from behind the stockade fence on the grassy knoll area. These findings have been disputed by other experts.

The Magic Bullet Theory: Theory proposed by the Warren Commission that the same shot that hit President Kennedy in his back and exited his throat, also hit Governor Connally and caused all of his wounds.

The President's Wounds: There is much controversy surrounding reports of how the President's wounds looked to the doctors who attended him in Dallas, and what the autopsy photos later showed.

The Zapruder Film: 8 mm film clip of the JFK assassination, taken by Abraham Zapruder.

Mexico City: Capital of Mexico. Oswald traveled there to get a temporary visa to Cuba shortly before he allegedly murdered President Kennedy in Dallas.

The Warren Commission: A congressional commission created to investigate the assassination of President Kennedy, headed by Supreme Court Chief Justice Earl Warren. The commission determined that Lee Oswald acted alone and that there was no evidence of a conspiracy.

The House Select Committee on Assassinations (HSCA): A congressional committee that reopened the investigation into the assassinations of President John F. Kennedy and Martin Luther King Jr. in 1976. This committee, headed by a former justice department staffer, Professor G. Robert Blakey, found there was evidence of a conspiracy behind both men's deaths, but failed to name any specific conspirators.

The Assassination Records Review Board: A board created by Congress to make sure all JFK assassination-related documents were released as soon as possible.

New Orleans: Lee Harvey Oswald's birthplace. Oswald's possible associates in New Orleans include a former airline pilot, David Ferrie, who had direct links to mafia boss, Carlos Marcello, and even stronger links to former FBI agent and private investigator, Guy Banister.

Thoughts on the Hereafter

"Where do you think President Kennedy went after he died?"

I was standing in the middle of Dealey Plaza, researching the JFK assassination case in 2008 when I was asked this question by a man I later came to know as a Christian apologist. Since I was researching the case, I assumed his question was a historical one, so I attempted to break down President Kennedy's trip to Parkland Hospital.

The man graciously stopped me, then asked more plainly whether I thought the president's soul went to heaven or to hell.

I told him I didn't know. I didn't think a lot about such things.

Then he looked me in the eyes and asked me where I thought I would go if I were to die that day.

I had no answer for that question. I knew more about our country's history than I did about my eternal destiny. The man kindly and compassionately explained the situation to me. I had sinned against God my entire life. He explained how Christ died to pay the price for my sins so that I would not be held accountable to God for my past action. He encouraged me to believe in Jesus as my Savior, turn from my sins and submit to His Word.

He wasn't rude or pushy. Instead, he just pointed toward God's love for me.

We prayed for my conversion right there on the grassy knoll, where more than 50 years before someone allegedly had taken a shot at the President of the United States. Then I watched that man walk away into the parking lot of the Sixth Floor Museum.

I didn't have a 'break down in tears' moment. The sky didn't split open and there were no angel choirs. But I can say that God began to change my heart. I now look back upon that moment with gratefulness for that man's courage to share the gospel of Christ with me.

What about you? Where will you go after you 'shuffle off this mortal coil' as Shakespeare would have it? As a researcher, I hope you have contemplated this issue, because nothing is more vital to your life than that question.

I am a Christian in a time where being a Christian is not as popular as it once was. That doesn't mean I think I'm better than anyone else, and it certainly doesn't mean I think I've arrived. Quite the opposite. I have struggles and I fail often. But I live my life knowing that the price for my sins has been paid in full.

Not long ago, I was a mess. I had no purpose in life. I was a hateful, ungrateful individual with a severe drug addiction. But God, in His mercy, came into my life and delivered me from that hopeless condition. I have never looked back.

There is no greater question than your eternal destination. There is no greater peace than trusting in Christ alone. That's why I encourage you to do the research. Consider your life. Are you a mess, like I was? Are you in need of a Savior? Where do you think President Kennedy went after he died? Where do you think you will go?

Special Thanks

I want to thank everyone who helped me complete this book. Thank you to all of the researchers who dedicated their personal time to interview with me. I would have been lost without your insights. Thank you to my friends and family who allowed me to use their time to research this book. Thank you for your recorder Darrian. Thank you Pastor Pete and Mrs. Kelli for always encouraging me to pursue my dreams. Thank you Mom for listening to my wild JFK theories throughout the years. Thank you God for changing my heart, and for providing a new life for me. I am nothing without the blood of your son, Jesus.

Also Available From

WordCrafts Press

Never Run a Dead Kata
by Rodney Boyd

Aerobics for the Mind
by Michael Potts, PhD

Why I Failed in the Music Business
and how NOT to follow in my footsteps
by Steve Grossman

Letters at Midnight
by Roland B. King

Uncommon Core
by Pauline Hawkins

Shameless Self Promotion
by Parker, Parker & Martin

A Scarlet Cord of Hope
By Sheryl Griffin

www.wordcrafts.net